Pocket
Puerto Rico

Reprinted from *Fodor's Caribbean '91*.

Fodor's Travel Publications, Inc.
New York and London

Fodor's Pocket Puerto Rico

Editor: Larry Peterson
Area Editor: Honey Naylor
Research: Todd Whitley
Art Director: Fabrizio La Rocca
Cartographer: David Lindroth
Illustrator: Karl Tanner
Cover Photograph: Martin Vloo/Uniphoto

Design: Vignelli Associates

Special Sales

Fodor's Travel Publications are available at special discounts for bulk purchases (100 copies or
more) for sales promotions or premiums. Special
editions, including personalized covers, ex-
cerpts of existing guides, and corporate im-
prints, can be created in large quantities for
special needs. For more information write to
Special Marketing, Fodor's Travel Publications,
201 East 50th St., New York, NY 10022. Inquiries from the United Kingdom should be sent to
Fodor's Travel Publications, 20 Vauxhall Bridge
Rd., London, England SW1V 2SA.

Contents

Foreword

Fodor's Pocket Puerto Rico is intended especially for the new or short-term visitor who wants a complete but concise account of the most exciting places to see and the most interesting things to do.

Those who plan to spend more time in the Caribbean, or seek additional information about areas of interest, will want to consult *Fodor's Caribbean* for in-depth coverage of the area.

While every care has been taken to assure the accuracy of the information in this guide, the passage of time will always bring change, and consequently the publisher cannot accept responsibility for errors that may occur.

All prices and opening times quoted here are based on information available to us at press time. Hours and admission fees may change, however, and the prudent traveler will avoid inconvenience by calling ahead.

Fodor's wants to hear about your travel experiences, both pleasant and unpleasant. When a hotel or restaurant fails to live up to its billing, let us know and we will investigate the complaint and revise our entries where the facts warrant it.

Send your letters to the editors of Fodor's Travel Publications, 201 E. 50th St., New York, NY 10022.

The Caribbean

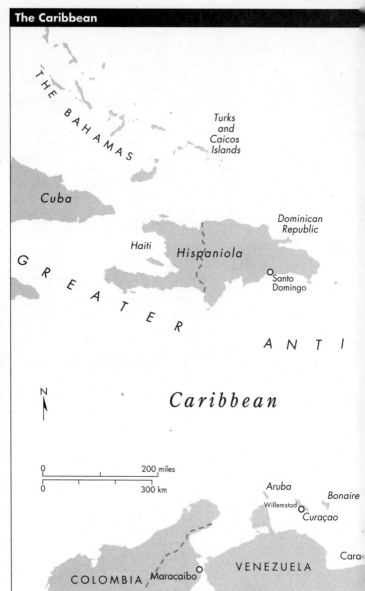

THE BAHAMAS

Turks
and
Caicos
Islands

Cuba

Dominican
Republic

Haiti Hispaniola

G R E A T E R

Santo
Domingo

A N T I

N

Caribbean

0   200 miles
0   300 km

Aruba

Bonaire

Willemstad Curaçao

COLOMBIA Maracaibo VENEZUELA Cara

ATLANTIC OCEAN

LEEWARD ISLANDS

San Juan
St. John
St. Thomas
Virgin Gorda
Tortola
Anguilla
St. Barthélemy
St. Maarten/
St. Martin
Saba
Barbuda
Puerto
Rico
St.
Croix
St. Eustatius
St. Kitts
Nevis
Montserrat
Antigua
Marie
Galante
Guadeloupe
Dominica
Martinique
Fort-de-France
St. Lucia
Barbados
Bridgetown
St. Vincent
The
Grenadines
St. George's
Grenada
Tobago
Bonaire
açao
Caracas
Trinidad

TILLES
Sea
LESSER ANTILLES
WINDWARD ISLANDS

Introduction

*by J.P.
MacBean*

Puerto Rico is so complex in its history and culture—so rich in the variety of its activities and attractions—that it would be a great mistake to think of this lovely island as simply another resort area. It is of course a wonderful playground—its beaches are sandy and properly palm fringed; its casinos, discos, and nightclubs quicken pulses; its hotels and *paradores* cater to both the jaded jet setter and the incurable romantic; and its restaurants pay homage to the cuisines of the world.

The decision that faces all visitors to Puerto Rico is what *type* of visit to have. The choices are numerous: a beach vacation in San Juan's fashionable Condado or Isla Verde areas; a stay in Old San Juan, whose narrow colonial streets and historic sites are easily explored on foot; a drive-around-the-island adventure, stopping in other Puerto Rican cities like Ponce and Mayagüez, a visit to a self-contained resort like Dorado Beach, Cerromar Beach, or Palmas del Mar; or a drive to a *parador* like Gripiñas, a former 19th-century coffee plantation in the hills above Ponce. Those who want to get away from it all can even hop a plane to one of Puerto Rico's offshore islands—Culebra or Vieques, for example.

First-time visitors will probably elect to stay in San Juan—in either the old or beachfront sections—and take day trips to various attractions like Luquillo Beach, El Yunque rain forest, Ponce ("The Pearl of the South"), Mayagüez on the western coast, and Arecibo Observatory and the Rio Camuey Cave Park in the northwestern section of the island.

Because of Puerto Rico's benevolent climate, the island is a popular vacation spot throughout the year. Nevertheless, the crowds tend to come during the late fall to early spring period, escaping the winter weather up north. Puerto Rico attracts a wide variety of visitors: vacationers and honeymooners on package plans, cruise passengers docking at San Juan's handsome old port, sun-seeking Canadians and vacationing college students, the rich and famous checking into luxury resorts like Dorado and Cerromar Beach, and sports lovers flying (or sailing) in for the golf, tennis, fishing, swimming, surfing, scuba diving, and horse racing. Although the sun, the sea, and the casinos are perhaps the biggest initial draws, most visitors leave with rave reviews for the warm and friendly people, the relaxed atmosphere throughout the island, the compelling history and culture, and the fascinating shops, galleries, and restaurants.

1 Essential Information

Before You Go

Tourist Information

Contact the **Puerto Rico Tourism Company** at the following addresses: 575 5th Ave., 23rd Floor, New York, NY 10017, tel. 212/599–6262 or 800/223–6530; 3228–I Quails Lake Village La., Norcross, GA 30093, tel. 404/564–9362; 233 N. Michigan Ave., Suite 2204, Chicago, IL 60601, tel. 312/861–0049; 3386 Van Horn 106, Trenton, MI 48183, tel. 313/676–2190; 3575 W. Cahuenga Blvd., Suite 248, Los Angeles, CA 90068, tel. 213/874–5991; Peninsula Bldg., Suite 903, 200 S.E. First St., Miami, FL 33131, tel. 305/381–8915; 2504 Marilyn Cir., Petaluma, CA 94952, tel. 707/762–3468; Box 2662, St. Louis, MO 63116, tel. 314/481–8216; Box 8053, Falls Church, VA 22041–8053, tel. 703/671–0930; or 11 Yorkville Ave., Suite 1003, Toronto, Ont., Canada M4W IL3, tel. 416/925–5587; Charles Ovington Sq., Suite 402, London, England SW3 ILN, tel. 71–589–5216.

Festivals and Seasonal Events

April Citron Harvest Festival.

May A 16th-century Dominican convent in San Juan is the setting for a week of music and dance performances known as *Semana de la Danza*.

June From all over the world, orchestras, choruses, and choirs converge on San Juan for Festival Casals.

December Although they hold a White Christmas Festival in Puerto Rico, you have little reason to fear snow in the Caribbean.

What to Pack

Pack light because baggage carts are scarce at airports and luggage restrictions are tight.

Clothing Dress on the islands is light and casual. Bring loose-fitting clothes made of natural fabrics to see you through days of heat and high humidity. Take a coverup for the beaches, not only to protect you from the sun, but also to wear to and from your hotel room. Bathing suits and immodest attire are frowned upon off the beach. A sun hat is advisable, but there's no need to pack one because inexpensive straw hats are available everywhere. For shopping and sightseeing, bring walking shorts, jeans, T-shirts, long-sleeve cotton shirts, slacks, and sundresses. Air-conditioning in hotels and restaurants often borders on the glacial, so bring a sweater or jacket for dining out. Evening wear is casual; jacket and tie is rarely required.

Miscellaneous It's advisable to wear a hat and sun-block lotion while sightseeing. Bring a spare pair of eye-glasses and sunglasses and an adequate supply of any prescription drugs you may need. You can probably find what you need in the pharmacies, but you may need a local doctor's prescription. Although you'll want an umbrella during the rainy season, you can pick up inexpensive ones locally. Leave the plastic or nylon raincoats at home; the high humidity makes them extremely uncomfortable. Bring suntan lotions and film from home in abundant supply; they're much more expensive on the islands. It's wise, too, to bring insect repellent, especially if you plan to walk through rain forests or visit during the rainy season.

Carry-on Passengers on U.S. airlines are limited to two
Luggage carry-on bags. For a bag you wish to store under the seat, the maximum dimensions are 9″ × 14″ × 22″. For bags that can be hung in a closet or on a luggage rack, the maximum dimensions are 4″ × 23″ × 45″. For bags you wish to store in an overhead bin, the maximum dimensions are 10″ × 14″ × 36″. Any item that exceeds the specified dimensions may be rejected as a carryon and taken as checked baggage. Keep in mind that an airline can adapt the rules to circumstances, so on an especially crowded flight don't be sur-prised if you are allowed only one carry-on bag.

In addition to the two carryons, you may bring aboard a handbag (pocketbook or purse); an overcoat or wrap; an umbrella; a camera; a rea-sonable amount of reading material; an infant bag; crutches, cane, braces, or other prosthetic device; and an infant/child safety seat (depend-ing upon space availability).

Foreign airlines have slightly different policies. They generally allow only one piece of carry-on luggage in tourist class, in addition to handbags and bags filled with duty-free goods. Passengers in first and business class may also be allowed to carry on one garment bag. It is best to call your airline to find out its current policy.

Checked Luggage Luggage allowances vary slightly from airline to airline. Many carriers allow three checked pieces; some allow only two. It is best to check before you go. In all cases, check-in luggage cannot weigh more than 70 pounds per piece or be larger than 62 inches (length + width + height).

Getting Money from Home

There are at least three ways to get money from home:

1) Have it sent through a large commercial bank with a branch on the island. The only drawback is that you must have an account with the bank; if not, you will have to go through your own bank and the process will be slower and more expensive.

2) Have it sent through **American Express**. If you are a cardholder, you can cash a personal check or a counter check at an American Express office for up to $1,000; $200 will be in cash and $800 in traveler's checks. There is a 1% commission on the traveler's checks. You can also get money through **American Express MoneyGram.** Through this service, you can receive up to $5,000 cash. It works this way: You call home and ask someone to go to an American Express office or an American Express MoneyGram agent located in a retail outlet and fill out an American Express MoneyGram. It can be paid for with cash or any major credit card. The person making the payment is given a reference number and telephones you with that number. The American Express MoneyGram agent calls an 800 number and authorizes the transfer of funds to an American Express office or participating agency. In most cases, the money is available immediately on a 24-hour basis. You pick it up by showing identification and giving the reference number. Fees vary according to the amount of money sent. For sending $300, the

fee is $30; for $5,000, $175. For the American Express MoneyGram location nearest your home, and to find out where the service is available in Puerto Rico, call 800/543–4080. You do not have to be a cardholder to use this service.

3) Have it sent through **Western Union** (tel. 800/325–6000). If you have a MasterCard or Visa, you can have money sent for any amount up to your credit limit. If not, have someone take cash or a certified cashier's check to a Western Union office. The money will be delivered in two business days to a bank near where you're staying. Fees vary with the amount of money sent and its destination. For Puerto Rico and the U.S. Virgin Islands, the rate is $47 for $1,000 and $37 for $500.

Cash Machines   Virtually all U.S. banks now belong to a network of Automatic Teller Machines (ATMs) that dispense cash 24 hours a day. There are eight major networks in the United States, and some banks belong to more than one. In the past year, two of the largest systems, Cirrus, which is owned by MasterCard, and Plus, which is affiliated with Visa, have extended their service to U.S. territories and to foreign cities that attract large numbers of tourist and business travelers. The Plus system, for example, already has outlets in Puerto Rico and the U.S. Virgin Islands and may be expanding to other islands in the Caribbean. Each network has a toll-free number you can call to locate its machines in a given city. The Cirrus number is 800/424–7787; the Plus number is 800/843–7587. Note that these cash cards are not issued automatically; they must be requested at your specific branch.

Cards issued by Visa, American Express, and MasterCard can also be used in ATMs, but the fees are usually higher than the fees on bank cards (and there is a daily interest charge on the loan). All three companies issue directories that list the national and international outlets that accept their cards. You can pick up a Visa or MasterCard directory at your local bank. For an American Express directory, call 800/CASH–NOW (this number can also be used for general inquiries). Contact your bank for information on fees and the amount of cash you can withdraw on any given day. Although each bank individually charges for taking money with the card, using your American Express, Visa, or MasterCard at an ATM can be cheaper than exchanging money in a bank because of variations in exchange rates.

Traveling with Film

If your camera is new, shoot and develop a few rolls of film before you leave home. Pack some lens tissue and an extra battery for your built-in light meter. Invest about $10 in a skylight filter and screw it onto the front of your lens. It will protect the lens and also reduce haze.

Film doesn't like hot weather. If you're driving in summer, don't store film in the glove compartment or on the shelf under the rear window. Put it behind the front seat on the floor, on the side opposite the exhaust pipe.

On a plane trip, never pack unprocessed film in check-in luggage; if your bags get X-rayed, you can say good-bye to your pictures. Always carry undeveloped film with you through security, and ask to have it inspected by hand. (It helps to isolate your film in a plastic bag, ready for quick inspection.) Inspectors at American airports are required by law to honor requests for hand inspection; abroad, you'll have to depend on the kindness of strangers.

The old airport scanning machines—still in use in some countries—use heavy doses of radiation that can turn a family portrait into an early morning fog. The newer models—used in all U.S. airports—are safe for anything from five to 500 scans, depending on the speed of your film. The effects are cumulative; you can put the same roll of film through several scans without worry. After five scans, though, you're asking for trouble.

If your film gets fogged and you want an explanation, send it to the **National Association of Photographic Manufacturers** (550 Mamaroneck Ave., Harrison, NY 10528). They will try to determine what went wrong. The service is free.

Staying Healthy

Few real hazards threaten the health of a visitor to Puerto Rico. Poisonous snakes are hard to find, and the small lizards that seem to have overrun the islands are harmless. The worst problem may well be a tiny predator, the "no see'um," a small sand fly that tends to appear after a rain, near wet or swampy ground, and around sunset. If you feel particularly vulnerable to insect bites, bring along a good repellent.

The worst problem tends to be sunburn or sunstroke. Even people who are not normally bothered by strong sun should head into this area with a long-sleeve shirt, a hat, and long pants or a beach wrap. These are essential for a day on a boat but are also advisable for midday at the beach. Also carry some sun-block lotion for nose, ears, and other sensitive areas such as eyelids, ankles, etc. Be sure to drink enough liquids. Above all, limit your sun time for the first few days until you become used to the heat.

Since health standards vary from island to island, it's best to inquire about the island you plan to visit before you go. No special shots are required for Puerto Rico. If you have a health problem that might require purchasing prescription drugs while in Puerto Rico, have your doctor write a prescription using the drug's generic name; brand names may be different.

The International Association for Medical Assistance to Travelers (IAMAT) is a worldwide organization offering a list of approved English-speaking doctors whose training meets British and American standards. Contact IAMAT for a list of physicians and clinics in the Caribbean that belong to this network. **In the United States:** 417 Center Street, Lewiston, NY 14092, tel. 716/754–4883. **In Canada:** 40 Regal Road, Guelph, Ontario N1K 1B5. **In Europe:** 57 Voirets, 1212 Grand–Lancy, Geneva, Switzerland. Membership is free.

Insurance

Travelers may seek insurance coverage in three areas: health and accident, lost luggage, and trip cancellation. Your first step is to review your existing health and home-owner policies. Some health insurance plans cover health expenses incurred while traveling, some home-owner policies cover luggage theft, and some major medical plans cover emergency transportation.

Health and Accident

Several companies offer coverage designed to supplement existing health insurance for travelers:

Carefree Travel Insurance (Box 310, 120 Mineola Blvd., Mineola, NY 11501, tel. 516/294–0220 or 800/343–3553) provides coverage for medical evacuation. It also offers 24-hour medical advice by phone, will help find English-speaking medical and legal assistance anywhere in the world, and offers direct payment to hospitals for emergency medical care.

Wallach and Company, Inc. (243 Church St., NW, Suite 100D, Vienna, VA 22180, tel. 703/281–9500 or 800/237–6615) offers comprehensive medical coverage, including emergency evacuation for trips of 10–90 days.

International SOS Assistance (Box 11568, Philadelphia, PA 19116, tel. 215/244–1500 or 800/523–8930) does not offer medical insurance but provides medical evacuation and repatriation services.

Travel Guard International, underwritten by Transamerica Occidental Life Companies (1100 Centerpoint Dr., Stevens Point, WI 54481, tel. 715/345–0505 or 800/782–5151), offers reimbursement for medical expenses with no deductibles or daily limits, and emergency evacuation services.

Lost Luggage

Luggage loss is usually covered as part of a comprehensive travel insurance package that includes personal accident, trip cancellation, and sometimes default and bankruptcy insurance. Several companies offer comprehensive policies:

Access America, Inc., a subsidiary of Blue Cross–Blue Shield (600 3rd Ave., Box 807, New York, NY 10163, tel. 212/490–5345 or 800/284–8300).

Near Services (1900 N. MacArthur Blvd., Suite 210, Oklahoma City, OK 73127, tel. 800/654–6700 or in Oklahoma City, 405/949–2500).

Travel Guard International (*see* Health and Accident Insurance, above).

Carefree Travel Insurance (*see* Health and Accident Insurance, above).

Luggage Insurance Airlines are responsible for lost or damaged property only up to $1,250 per passenger on domestic flights, and $9.07 per pound ($20 per kilo) for checked baggage on international flights, and up to $400 per passenger for unchecked baggage on international flights. If you're carrying valuables, either take them with you on the airplane or purchase additional insurance for lost luggage. Some airlines will issue additional insurance when you check in, but many do not. One that does is American Airlines. Rates for both domestic and international flights are $1 for every $100 valuation, with a maximum of $400 valuation per passenger. Hand luggage is not included.

Insurance for lost, damaged, or stolen luggage is available through travel agents or directly through various insurance companies. Two companies that issue luggage insurance are **Tele-Trip** (P.O. Box 31685, 3201 Farnam St., Omaha, NE 68131, tel. 800/228–9792), a subsidiary of Mutual of Omaha, and **The Travelers Insurance Co.** (Ticket and Travel Dept., 1 Tower Square, Hartford, CT 06183, tel. 203/277–0111 or 800/243–3174). Tele-Trip, which operates sales booths at airports and also issues policies through travel agents, insures checked luggage for up to 180 days and for $500–$3,000 valuation. For one–three days, the rate for a $500 valuation is $8.25; for 180 days, $100. The Travelers Insurance Co. insures checked or hand luggage for $500–$2,000 valuation per person, also for a maximum of 180 days. Rates for up to five days for $500 valuation are $10; for 180 days, $85. Both companies offer the same rates on domestic and international flights. Check the travel pages of your local newspaper for the names of other companies that insure luggage.

Before you go, itemize the contents of each bag in case you need to file an insurance claim. Be certain to put your home address on each piece of luggage, including carry-on bags. If your luggage is stolen and later recovered, the airline must deliver the luggage to your home free of charge.

Trip Cancellation Flight insurance is often included in the price of a ticket when paid for with an American Express, Visa, or other major credit and charge cards. It is usually included in combination travel insurance packages available from most tour operators, travel agents, and insurance agents.

Insurance for British Travelers We recommend that to cover health and motoring mishaps, you insure yourself with **Europ Assisance** (252 High St., Croyden, Surrey CRO INF, tel 01/680–1234).

It is also wise to take out insurance to cover the loss of luggage (although check that such loss isn't already covered in any existing homeowner's policies you may have). Trip-cancellation insurance is another wise buy. **The Association of British Insurers** (Aldermary House, Queen St., London EC4N ITT, tel. 01/248–4477) will give comprehensive advice on all aspects of vacation insurance.

Student and Youth Travel

The **International Student Identity Card** (ISIC) entitles students to special fares on local transportation and discounts at museums, theaters, sports events, and many other attractions. If purchased in the United States, the $10 ISIC also includes $2,000 in emergency medical insurance, plus $100 a day for up to 60 days of hospital coverage and a collect-call phone number to use for emergencies. Apply to the **Council on International Educational Exchange (CIEE)** (205 E. 42nd St., New York, NY 10017, tel. 212/661–1450). In Canada, the ISIC is available for C$7.50 from the Federation of Students–Services (171 College St., Toronto, Ont. M5T 1P7).

Council Travel, a CIEE subsidiary, is the foremost U.S. student travel agency, specializing in low-cost charters and serving as the exclusive U.S. agent for many student airfare bargains and student tours. (CIEE's 80-page *Student Travel Catalog* and "Council Charter" brochure are available free from any Council Travel office in the United States; enclose $1 postage if ordering by mail.) In addition to the CIEE headquarters at 205 East 42nd Street and a branch office at 35 West 8th Street in New York City (tel. 212/254–2525), there are Council Travel offices in Berkeley, La Jolla, Long Beach, Los Angeles, San Diego, San Francisco, and Sherman Oaks, CA; New Haven, CT; Washington, DC; Atlanta, GA; Chicago and Evanston, IL; New Orleans, LA; Amherst, Boston, and Cambridge, MA; Minneapolis, MN; Portland, OR; Providence, RI; Austin and Dallas, TX; Seattle, WA; and Milwaukee, WI.

The **Educational Travel Center** (438 N. Frances St., Madison, WI 55703, tel. 608/256–5551) is another student travel specialist worth contacting for information on student tours, bargain fares, and bookings.

Students who would like to work abroad should contact **CIEE's Work Abroad Department** (205 E. 42nd St., New York, NY 10017) tel. 212/661–1414, ext. 1130. The council arranges various types of paid and voluntary work experiences overseas for up to six months. CIEE also sponsors study programs in Latin America and publishes many books of interest to the student traveler: these include *Work, Study, Travel Abroad; The Whole World Handbook* ($9.95 plus $1.00 book-rate postage or $2.50 first-class postage) and *Volunteer! The Comprehensive Guide to Voluntary Service in the U.S. and Abroad* ($6.95 plus $1.00 book-rate postage or $2.50 first-class postage).

The Information Center at the **Institute of International Education** (809 UN Plaza, New York, NY 10017, tel. 212/984–5413) has reference books, foreign university catalogues, study-abroad brochures, and other materials that may be consulted by students and nonstudents alike, free of charge. The Information Center is open weekdays 10–4. For a current list of IIE publications, prices, and ordering information, write to Institute of International Education Books at the above address. Books must be purchased by mail or in person; telephone orders are not accepted. General information on IIE programs and services is available from the institute's regional offices in Atlanta, Chicago, Denver, Houston, San Francisco, and Washington, DC.

Traveling with Children

Publications *Family Travel Times* is an 8- to 12-page newsletter published 10 times a year by **TWYCH** (Travel with Your Children, 80 8th Ave., New York, NY 10011, tel. 212/206–0688). The $35 yearly subscription includes access to back issues and twice-weekly opportunities to call in for specific information. Send $1 for a sample issue. The September issue is always devoted entirely to the Caribbean.

Great Vacations with Your Kids, (second edition) by Dorothy Jordan (founder of TWYCH) and Marjorie Cohen, offers complete advice on planning a trip with children (toddlers to teens) and details everything from city vacations to adventure vacations to child-care resources ($12.95, E.P. Dutton, 2 Park Ave., New York, NY 10016).

"Kids and Teens in Flight" and "Fly Rights" are U.S. Department of Transportation brochures with information on special services for young travelers. To order free copies, call 202/366–2220.

Accommodations In addition to offering family discounts and spe-
Hotels cial rates for children (for example, some large hotel chains do not charge extra for children under 12 if they stay in their parents' room), many hotels and resorts arrange for baby-sitting services and run a variety of special children's programs. The following list is representative of the kinds of services and activities offered by some of the major chains and resorts. It is by no means exhaustive. If you are going to be traveling with your children, be sure to check with your travel agent for more information or ask hotel representatives about children's programs when you are making reservations.

In **Puerto Rico,** the **Hyatt Regency Cerromar Beach** and the **Hyatt Dorado Beach Hotel** operate a complimentary camp for children age 5–12 all summer, at Christmastime and at Easter. One of the camp's main attractions is a meandering, free-form freshwater pool with waterfalls, bridges, and a 187-foot water slide. The camp's staff includes bilingual college-age counselors. For more information, call 800/233–1234. The El

San Juan in Puerto Rico (tel. 800/468–2818) has a program for children in the same age group that features swimnastics, treasure hunts, beach walks, exercise classes, tennis, and an always-open game room.

Villa Rentals **At Home Abroad, Inc.** (405 E. 56th St., Suite 6H, New York, NY 10022, tel. 212/421–9165).

Villas International (71 W. 23rd St., Suite 1402, New York, NY 10010, tel. 212/929–7585 or 800/221–2260).

Hideaway International (Box 1270, Littleton, MA 01460, tel. 508/486–8955).

Villas and Apartments Abroad (420 Madison Ave., Room 305, New York, NY 10017, tel. 212/759–1025).

Home Exchange Exchanging homes is a surprisingly low-cost way to enjoy a vacation abroad, especially a long one. The largest home-exchange service, **International Home Exchange Service** (Box 3975, San Francisco, CA 94119, tel. 415/435–3497) publishes three directories a year. Membership, which costs $35, entitles you to one listing and all three directories. Photos of your property cost an additional $8.50, and listing a second home costs $10. A good choice for domestic home exchange, **Vacation Exchange Club, Inc.** (12006 111th Ave., Unit 12, Youngstown, AZ 85363, tel. 602/972–2186), publishes one directory in February and a supplement in April. Membership is $24.70 per year, for which you receive one listing. Photos cost another $9; listing a second home costs $6. **Loan-a-Home** (2 Park La., Mount Vernon, NY 10552) is popular with the academic community on sabbatical and with businesspeople on temporary assignment. There's no annual membership fee or charge for listing your home, however one directory and a supplement costs $30. Loan-a-Home publishes two directories (in December and June) and two supplements (in March and September) each year. All four books cost $40 per year.

Getting There All children, including infants, must have a passport for foreign travel; family passports are no longer issued. (For more information, *see* the Passports and Visas sections in the individual chapters.)

On international flights, children under age 2 not occupying a seat pay 10% of adult fare; on domestic flights, they travel free. Various discounts apply to children age 2–12. Reserve a seat behind the bulkhead of the plane, which offers more legroom and can usually fit a bassinet (supplied by the airline). At the same time, inquire about special children's meals or snacks, which are offered by most airlines. (See "TWYCH's Airline Guide" in the February 1990 issue of *Family Travel Times* for a rundown on children's services furnished by 46 airlines; an update is planned for February 1992.) Ask your airline in advance if you can bring aboard your child's car seat. (For the pamphlet *Child/Infant Safety Seats Acceptable for Use in Aircraft*, contact the Community and Consumer Liaison Division, APA200, Federal Aviation Administration, Washington, DC 20591, tel. 202/267–3479.)

Hints for Disabled Travelers

The **Information Center for Individuals with Disabilities** (Fort Point Place, 1st floor, 27–43 Wormwood St., Boston, MA 02210, tel. 617/727–5540) offers useful problem-solving assistance, including lists of travel agents who specialize in tours for the disabled.

Moss Rehabilitation Hospital Travel Information Service (12th St. and Tabor Rd., Philadelphia, PA 19141, tel. 215/329–5715) provides information on tourist sights, transportation, and accommodations in destinations around the world. There is a small fee.

Mobility International U.S.A. (Box 3551, Eugene, OR 97403, tel. 503/343–1284) is a membership organization with a $20 annual fee offering information on accommodations, organized study, and so forth around the world.

The **Society for the Advancement of Travel for the Handicapped** (26 Court St., Penthouse Suite, Brooklyn, NY 11242, tel. 718/858–5483) offers access information. Annual membership costs $40, $25 for senior travelers and students. Send $2 and a stamped, self-addressed envelope for a list of tour operators who arrange travel for the disabled.

Travel Industry and Disabled Exchange (TIDE, 5435 Donna Ave., Tarzana, CA 91356, tel. 818/ 343–6339) is an industry-based organization with a $15-per-person annual membership fee. Members receive a quarterly newsletter and a directory of travel agencies for the disabled.

Publications Twin Peaks Press publishes a number of useful resources: *Travel for the Disabled* ($9.95), *Directory of Travel Agencies for the Disabled* ($12.95), and *Wheelchair Vagabond* ($9.95 paperback, $14.95 hardcover). Order through your local bookstore or directly from the publisher (Twin Peaks Press, Box 129, Vancouver, WA 98666, tel. 206/694–2462). Add $2 per book postage and $1 for each additional book.

Access to the World: A Travel Guide for the Handicapped, by Louise Weiss, is a well-known and trusted guidebook that has recently been updated (Henry Holt & Co., $12.95 plus $2 shipping, tel. 800/247–3912 to order; include order number 0805001417).

"**Fly Rights,**" a free U.S. Department of Transportation brochure, offers airline access information for the handicapped. To order, call 202/ 366–2220.

Accommodations In the more popular destinations throughout the Caribbean, the specific needs of the disabled are now often being taken into consideration when new hotels are built or existing properties are renovated. A number of cruise ships, such as the *QE II* and the Norwegian Caribbean Line's *Seward,* have also recently adapted some of their cabins to meet the needs of disabled passengers. To make sure that a given establishment provides adequate access, ask about specific facilities when making a reservation or consider booking through a travel agent who specializes in travel for the disabled (*see* above).

Hints for Older Travelers

The **American Association of Retired Persons** (AARP, 1990 K St., NW, Washington, DC 20049, tel. 202/872–4700) has two programs for independent travelers: (1) *The Purchase Privilege Program*, which offers discounts on hotels, airfare, car rentals, TV rentals, and sightseeing; and (2) the *AARP Motoring Plan*, which furnishes emergency aid (road service) and trip-routing information for an annual fee of $33.95 per person or married couple. The AARP also arranges group tours through **Olson-Travel-world** (100 N. Sepulveda Blvd., 10th Floor, El Segundo, CA 90245, tel. 213/615–0711 or 800/421–2255). As of 1991, group tours will be arranged by **American Express Vacations.** AARP members must be at least 50 years old. Annual dues are $5 per person or per couple.

If you're planning to use an AARP or other senior-citizen identification card to obtain a reduced hotel rate, mention it at the time you make your reservation rather than when you check out. At restaurants, show your card to the maître d' before you're seated; discounts may be limited to certain set menus, days, or hours. Your AARP card will identify you as a retired person but will not ensure a discount in all hotels and restaurants. When renting a car, remember that economy cars, priced at promotional rates, may cost less than the cars that are available with your ID card.

The **National Council of Senior Citizens** (925 15th St., NW, Washington, DC 20005, tel. 202/347–8800) is a nonprofit advocacy group with some 5,000 local clubs across the country. Annual membership is $12 per person or per couple. Members receive a monthly newspaper with travel information and an ID for reduced rates on hotels and car rentals.

Mature Outlook (6001 N. Clark St., Chicago, IL 60660, tel. 800/336–6330), a subsidiary of Sears, Roebuck, & Co., is a travel club for people over 50 years of age, offering hotel discounts and a bimonthly newsletter to its 800,000 members. Annual membership is $9.95 per person or couple. Instant membership is available at participating Holiday Inns.

Elderhostel (80 Boylston St., Suite 400, Boston, MA 02116, tel. 617/426–7788) is an innovative educational program for people 60 or over (only one member of a traveling couple has to qualify). Participants live in dormitories on some 1,200 campuses around the world. Mornings are devoted to lectures and seminars, afternoons to sightseeing and field trips. The fee for a trip includes room, board, tuition (in the United States and Canada) and round-trip transportation (overseas). Special scholarships in the United States and Canada are available for those who qualify financially. A catalogue of courses is free for a year *and* if you participate in a course; $10 a year after that if you don't.

Publications   *The International Health Guide for Senior Citizen Travelers,* by Dr. W. Robert Lange, MD, is available for $4.95, and *The Senior Citizens Guide to Budget Travel in the United States and Canada,* by Paige Palmer, is available for $4.95, plus $1 for shipping from Pilot Books (103 Cooper St., Babylon, NY 11702, tel. 516/422–2225).

The Discount Guide for Travelers over 55, by Caroline and Walter Weintz, lists helpful addresses, package tours, reduced rate car rentals, etc., in the United States and abroad. To order, send $7.95 plus $1.50 for shipping to Penguin USA/NAL, Cash Sales (Bergenfield Order Department, 120 Woodbine St., Bergenfield, NJ 07621, tel. 800/526–0275; include order number ISBN 0-525-483-58-6).

"**Fly Rights**" (tel. 202/366–2220), a free brochure published by the U.S. Department of Transportation, offers information on airline services available to elderly passengers.

Arriving and Departing

By Plane

The Luis Muñoz Marín International Airport east of downtown San Juan is the Caribbean hub for **American Airline** (tel. 800/433–7300). American has daily nonstop flights from New York and Dallas, and flies from Chicago via New York. **Delta** (tel. 800/221–1212) has direct service from Atlanta, Los Angeles, and Orlando; **Eastern** (tel. 800/327–8376) flies from Atlanta and Miami; and **TWA** (tel. 800/892–4141) flies from New York and St. Louis. In late 1989, **Pan Am** began serving San Juan from Miami, and **USAir** began daily nonstop service from Philadelphia and Charlotte, NC. Foreign carriers include **Air France** (tel. 800/237–2747), **British Airways** (tel.

800/247–9297), **BWIA** (tel. 800/327–7401), **Iberia** (tel. 800/772–4642), **LACSA** (tel. 800/225–2272), **LIAT** (tel. 809/791–3838), **Lufthansa** (tel. 800/645–3880), and **VIASA** (tel. 800/327–5454).

From the Airport **Airport Limousine Service** (tel. 809/791–4745) provides minibus service to hotels in the Isla Verde, Condado, and Old San Juan areas at basic fares of $1, $1.50, and $1.75, respectively; the fares, which are set by the Public Service Commission, can vary, depending upon time of day and number of passengers. Limousines of **Dorado Transport Service** (tel. 809/796–1214) serve hotels and villas in the Dorado area for $12 per person with a minimum of four passengers. Taxi fare from the airport to Isla Verde is about $5; to the Condado area, $8–$10; and to Old San Juan, $10–$12.

Passports and Visas

Puerto Rico is a Commonwealth of the United States and U.S. citizens do not need passports to visit the island. British citizens must have a passport and visa. Canadian citizens need proof of citizenship (preferably a passport).

Customs and Duties

U.S. citizens need not clear customs or immigration when traveling to or from Puerto Rico. However, when you depart, your luggage will be inspected by the U.S. Agriculture Department as there are prohibitions against taking certain fruits and plants into the United States.

British travelers returning to the United Kingdom (17 or over) may take home: (1) 200 cigarettes or 100 cigarillos or 50 cigars or 250 grams of tobacco; (2) 2 liters of table wine and (a) 1 liter of alcohol over 22% by volume (most spirits), (b) 2 liters of alcohol under 22% by volume (fortified or sparkling wine), or (c) 2 more liters of table wine; (3) 50 grams of perfume and ¼ liter of toilet water; and (4) other goods upt to a value of £32.

Language

The official language is Spanish, but almost everyone in and around San Juan speaks English. If you plan to rent a car and travel around the island, take along a Spanish phrase book.

Precautions

San Juan, like any other big city and major tourist destination, has its share of crime, so guard your wallet or purse on the city streets. Puerto Rico's beaches are open to the public, and muggings occur at night even on the beaches of the posh Condado and Isla Verde tourist hotels. Don't leave anything unattended on the beach. Leave your valuables in the hotel safe, and stick to the fenced-in beach areas of your hotel. Always lock your car and stash valuables and luggage out of sight. Avoid deserted beaches day or night.

Staying in Puerto Rico

Important Addresses

Tourist Information: The government-sponsored **Puerto Rico Tourism Company** (tel. 809/721–2400) is an excellent source for maps, brochures, and other printed guide materials. Pick up a free copy of *¿Qué Pasa?* the official visitors guide.

Information offices are located at **Luis Muñoz Marín International Airport,** Isla Verde (tel. 809/791–1014 or 809/791–2551); **El Centro Convention Center,** Condado (tel. 809/723–3135 or 809/722–1513); **301 Calle San Justo,** Old San Juan (tel. 809/721–2400), and **La Casita,** near Pier One in Old San Juan (tel. 809/722–1709). Out on the island, information offices are located in **Ponce** (Casa Armstrong-Poventud, Plaza, Las Delicias, tel. 809/840–5695); **Aguadilla** (Rafael Hernandez Airport, tel. 809/890–3315); and each town's city hall on the main plaza, open weekdays from 8 AM to noon and 1 to 4:30 PM.

Emergencies   **Police:** Call 809/343–2020.

Medical Emergency: Call 809/343–2550.

Hospitals: Hospitals in the Condado/Santurce area with 24-hour emergency rooms are **Ashford Memorial Community Hospital** (1451 Ashford

Ave., tel. 809/721–2160) and **San Juan Health Center** (200 De Diego Ave., tel. 809/725–0202).

Pharmacies: In San Juan, **Walgreen's** (1130 Ashford Ave., tel. 809/725–1510) is a 24-hour pharmacy. In Mayagüez there is another Walgreen's (16 Calle McKinley, tel. 809/833–6742), but it is not open 24 hours.

Currency

The U.S. dollar is the official currency of Puerto Rico.

Taxes and Service Charges

Hotels collect a 6% government tax on room charges. There is no departure tax.

Some hotels impose a 10% service charge. In restaurants, a 10%–15% tip is expected.

Guided Tours

Old San Juan can be seen either on a self-guided walking tour or on the free trolley. To explore the rest of the city and the island, consider renting a car. (We do, however, recommend a guided tour of the vast El Yunque rain forest.) If you'd rather not do your own driving, there are several tour companies you can call. Most San Juan hotels have a tour desk that can make arrangements for you. The standard half-day tours (at $10–$15) are of Old and New San Juan, Old San Juan and the Bacardi Rum Plant, Luquillo Beach and El Yunque rain forest. All-day tours ($15–$30) include a trip to Ponce, a day at El Comandante Racetrack, or a combined tour of the city and El Yunque rain forest.

Some of the leading tour operators are **Borinquén Tours, Inc.** (tel. 809/725–4990), **Gray Line of Puerto Rico** (tel. 809/727–8080), **Normandie Tours, Inc.** (tel. 809/725–6990 or 809/722–6308), **Rico Suntours** (tel. 809/722–2080 or 809/722–6090), and **United Tour Guides** (tel. 809/725–7605 or 809/723–5578). **Cordero Caribbean Tours** (tel. 809/799–6002) does tours (at hourly rates) out on the island in air-conditioned limousines.

Getting Around

Taxis Metered cabs authorized by the Public Service Commission (tel. 809/751–5050) charge an 80¢ drop and 10¢ for each additional ⅛ mile. There is a 50¢ charge per suitcase. Waiting time is $8 per hour.

Buses The **Metropolitan Bus Authority** (tel. 809/767–7979) operates the buses (or *guaguas)* that thread through San Juan. The fare is 25¢, and the buses run in exclusive lanes, *against the traffic* on major thoroughfares, stopping at upright yellow posts marked *Parada* or *Parada de Guaguas.* The main terminals downtown are at Plaza Colón and the Catano Ferry Terminal.

Públicos Public cars *(públicos)* with license plates ending with "P" or "PD" scoot to towns throughout the island, stopping in each town's main plaza. The five-passenger cars operate primarily during the day, with routes and fares fixed by the Public Service Commission. In San Juan, the main terminals are at the airport and on the waterfront in Old San Juan.

Trolleys If your feet fail you in Old San Juan, climb aboard the free open-air trolleys that rumble and roller-coast through the narrow streets. Departures are from La Puntilla and from the marina, but you can board them anywhere along the route.

Motor Coaches The **Puerto Rico Motor Coach Co.** (tel. 809/725–2460) makes daily runs between San Juan and Mayagüez, with stops at Arecibo and Aguadilla. A bus leaves San Juan every two hours, from 6 to 6, for a one-way fare of $6. Be sure to reserve in advance.

Ferries A round-trip ride between Old San Juan and Catano costs a mere 20¢. The ferry runs every half hour from 6:15 AM to 10 PM. The 400-passenger ferries of the **Fajardo Port Authority** (tel. 809/863–0705 or 800/462–2005) make the 80-minute trip twice daily between Fajardo and Vieques (one way $2 adults, $1 children), the one-hour run between Fajardo and Culebra daily (one way $2.25 adults, $1 children), and the half-hour trip between Vieques and Culebra on

Saturday, Sunday, Monday, and holidays (one way $2 adults, $1 children).

Rental Cars U.S. driver's licenses are valid in Puerto Rico for three months. All major U.S. car-rental agencies are represented on the island, including **Avis** (tel. 809/721–4499), **Hertz** (tel. 809/791–0840), **Budget** (tel. 809/791–3685), and **Thrifty** (tel. 809/791–4241). Prices start at $19.95 (plus insurance), with unlimited mileage. Most car rentals have shuttle service to or from the airport and the pickup point. If you plan to drive across the island, arm yourself with a good map and be aware that there are many unmarked roads up in the mountains. Many service stations in the central mountains do not take credit cards. Speed limits are posted in miles, distances in kilometers, and gas prices in liters.

Planes **Vieques Air-Link** (tel. 809/722–3736) flies from the Isla Grande Airport to Vieques and to Culebra, with each trip costing about $25 one way.

Telephones and Mail

The area code for Puerto Rico is 809. Since Puerto Rico uses U.S. postage stamps and has the same mail rates (17¢ for a postcard, 25¢ for a first-class letter), you can save time by bringing stamps with you. Post offices in major Puerto Rico cities offer Express Mail next-day service to the U.S. mainland and to Puerto Rico destinations.

Opening and Closing Times

Shops are open from 9 to 6 (from 9 to 9 during Christmas holidays). Banks are open weekdays from 8:30 to 2:30 and Saturday from 9:45 to noon.

Cruises

Cruising the Caribbean is perhaps the most relaxed and convenient way to tour this beautiful part of the world. A cruise offers all the benefits of island-hopping without the inconvenience. For example, a cruise passenger packs and unpacks only once and is not bound by flight schedules, tour-bus schedules, and "non schedules" of fellow travelers.

Cruise ships usually call at several Caribbean ports on a single voyage. Thus, a cruise passenger experiences and savors the mix of nationalities and cultures of the Caribbean, as well as the variety of sightseeing opportunities, the geographic and topographic characteristics, and the ambience of each of the islands. A cruise passenger tries out each island on his or her cruise itinerary and has the opportunity to select favorites for in-depth discovery on a later visit.

As a vacation, a cruise offers total peace of mind. All important decisions are made long before boarding the ship. For example, the itinerary is set in advance, and the costs are known ahead of time and are all-inclusive. There is no additional charge for accommodations, entertainment, or recreational activities. All meals are included, and (surprise!) there are no prices on the menu. A cruise ship is a floating Caribbean resort; each passenger gets to know the cruise staff and sits back and relaxes while he or she enjoys the consistency of service and experience.

Fly-and-Cruise

Several cruise lines offer attractive fly-and-cruise options, which give passengers the option of flying first to a warm-weather port like Miami or San Juan and boarding the ship there. The airfare is built into the rate, so the cost of the total package is usually higher than the cost of cruise-only packages that cover comparable distances at sea. In most cases, however, the airplus-cruise rate will be lower than round-trip airfare to the ship's pier.

When to Go

Cruise ships sail the Caribbean year-round—the waters are almost always calm, and the prevailing breezes keep temperatures fairly steady. Tropical storms are most likely in September, October, and November, but modern navigational equipment warns ships of impending foul weather, and, if necessary, cruise lines vary their itineraries to avoid storms.

Cruises are in high demand—and therefore also higher priced—during the standard vacation times in midsummer to early fall and around

Easter. Some very good bargains are usually available during the immediate post-vacation periods such as fall to mid-December, early spring, and the first few weeks after the Christmas and New Year's holidays. Christmas sailings are usually quite full and are priced at a premium.

Choosing a Cabin

Write to the cruise line or ask your travel agent for a ship's plan. This elaborate layout, with all cabin numbers noted, may seem overwhelming at first, but closer inspection will show you all facilities available on all decks (the higher the deck, the higher the prices). Outside cabins have dramatic portholes that contribute to the romance of cruising, but even if they aren't sealed shut, most provide no more than a view of the surrounding deck. Inside cabins are less expensive, but check the plan—you don't want to be over the kitchen, over the engine room, or next to the elevators if you want quiet. Then check on the facilities offered. Those prone to motion sickness would do best in a cabin at midship, on one of the lower decks. Cabins in the center of the ship are the most stable, and the higher you go, the more motion you'll experience. Look over the less-expensive cabins that have upper and lower berths, those that have bathtubs in addition to showers, and the luxury suites, which can still provide all the accoutrements of a voyage across the sea.

Tipping

Even though some of the liners advertise a no-tipping policy, be aware that most of the ship's service personnel depend on tips for their livelihood. There is no hard-and-fast rule about who gets what, but if you think of services rendered on board as you would at resort hotels, bars, and restaurants, you'll come close. It is customary to tip the cabin steward, the dining-room waiter, the maître d', the wine steward, and the bartender. Gratuities to other ship's personnel are usually given the night before the voyage ends.

Shore Excursions

Tour options are typically posted on the bulletin board near the purser's office a day before arrival at your port of call. If the ship is in port for a full day, you might choose to join a tour offered by one of the local tour companies or to rent a car and explore on your own.

Cruise Lines

To find out which ships are sailing where and when they depart, contact the **Caribbean Tourism Association** (20 E. 46th St., New York, NY 10017, tel. 212/682–0435). The CTA carries up-to-date information about cruise lines that sail to its member nations. Travel agencies are also a good source; they stock brochures and catalogues issued by most of the major lines and usually have the latest information about prices, departure dates, and itineraries. The **Cruise Lines International Association** publishes a useful pamphlet entitled *Answers to the Most Asked Questions about Cruising;* to order a copy send a stamped, self-addressed envelope to CLIA (17 Battery Pl., Suite 631, New York, NY 10004).

American Canadian Caribbean Line (Box 368, Warren, RI 02885, tel. 800/556–7450).
Bermuda Star Line (1086 Teaneck Rd., Teaneck, NJ 07666, tel. 800/237–5361).
Carnival Cruise Lines (5225 N.W. 87th Ave., Miami, FL 33178, tel. 800/327–9501; in FL, 800/432–5424).
Chandris Fantasy Cruises (900 3rd Ave., New York, NY 10022, tel. 212/750–0044, 800/621–3446, or 800/432–4132 in FL).
Clipper Cruise Line (7711 Bonhomme Ave., St. Louis, MO 63105, tel. 800/325–0010; in MO, 314/727–2929).
Commodore Cruise Line (1007 North America Way, Miami, FL 33132, tel. 800/327–5617 or 800/432–6793 in FL).
Costa Cruises (World Trade Center, 80 S.W. 8th St., Miami, FL 33130, tel. 305/358–7325 or 800/462–6782).
Cunard (555 5th Ave., New York, NY 10017, tel. 800/5–CUNARD).
Holland America (300 Elliot Ave. W, Seat-

tle, WA 98119, tel. 206/281–3535 or 800/426–0327).

Norwegian Cruise Lines (95 Merrick Way, Coral Gables, FL 33134, tel. 305/447–9660 or 800/327–3090).

Ocean Cruise Lines (1510 S.E. 17th St., Ft. Lauderdale, FL 33316, tel. 305/764–3500, 800/556–8850 on the East Coast, or 800/338–1700 on the West Coast).

Ocean Quest International (512 S. Peters St., New Orleans, LA 70130, tel. 800/338–3483).

Princess Cruises (10100 Santa Monica Blvd., Los Angeles, CA 90067, tel. 213/553–1666, 800/421–0522).

Royal Caribbean Cruise Line (903 South America Way, Miami, FL 33132, tel. 305/379–2601 or 800/327–6700).

Royal Viking Line (95 Merrick Way, Coral Gables, FL 33134, tel. 305/447–9660 or 800/422–8000).

Seabourn Cruise Line (55 Francisco St., San Francisco, CA 94133, tel. 415/391–7444 or 800/351–9595; 800/527–0999 in Canada).

Sun Line Cruises (1 Rockefeller Plaza, New York, NY 10020, tel. 212/397–6400 or 800/445–6400).

Windjammer Barefoot Cruises (Box 120, Miami Beach, FL 33119, tel. 305/672–6453 or 800/327–2601; in Canada 800/233–2603).

2 Portrait of Puerto Rico

City of Light

by Pete Hamill

Pete Hamill is a columnist for the New York Post *and* Esquire *magazine. His most recent novel is* Loving Women. *He is currently working on a screenplay about the Spanish-American War.*

The light is always yellow in the morning streets. Even in the soft, drizzling rains of summer or the fierce, wind-driven storms of early fall, I feel bathed in that luminous yellow light. It seeps from the walls of the old houses—a light formed by the centuries, an antique light, a light that once held conquistadores and slaves, sugar kings and freebooters, the light of old gold and vanished supremacies—the light of San Juan.

When I say San Juan, I don't mean that great urban sprawl, with its population of more than a million, that makes up the modern capital of the island of Puerto Rico. That San Juan, with its office towers and traffic jams, raw concrete-block factories and heartless condominia, is just another city of the 20th century. When I think of San Juan, I mean the old town, called San Juan Antiguo by the formal, but more affectionately referred to as Viejo San Juan by those who know it and love it and have been warmed by its yellow light.

My San Juan, the old town I first saw in the late 1950s and have been visiting ever since, fills a mere seven square blocks on a promontory hooked around to face the great harbor that made the Spanish christen this island Rich Port. Across the centuries, it has been battered by unnamed tropical storms, and, in 1989, felt the power of Hurricane Hugo. But Viejo San Juan endures.

Whenever I visit Puerto Rico, arriving on a screaming jet at the airport in Isla Verde, I always go first to the old town. It centers me, in an island society that is too often culturally and politically schizophrenic. It grants me a sense of proportion. The modern city vanishes and much of the 20th century goes with it. Few places on this earth make me as happy.

The past is part of the reason. In many American cities now, we seem to be living in an eternal present tense, as insubstantial as the images on television screens. Too many events flash across our minds in unconnected fragments; today's crises are forgotten tomorrow; we hear too much and see too much and never listen for the whispering of ghosts. But there has been a San Juan since 1521, one hundred years before the first Dutchman mortared two bricks together to begin making New York. When the American Revolution began, San Juan had been there for 255 years.

So it is no accident that when I walk from Plaza Colón (with its statue of Columbus disguised as Dean Rusk) into Calle San Francisco, my sense of time shifts. The past asserts itself and I am reminded that for a long time before the rise of the United States this was a Spanish-speaking hemisphere. I hear the conversations of Puerto Ricans, delivered in the staccato-rhythms of port people, full of jokes and innuendo and untranslatable local words. The air is thick with vowels. From the old mortar of the walls, the past murmurs: Wait, slow down, listen, have a glass of rum, and remember old sins, the folly of man, the futility of despair.

Columbus discovered America in 1492, and on his second voyage the following year, the Admiral of the Ocean Sea landed at the site of the present town of Aguadilla on the northwest coast of the island. There were then about 30,000 Taino Indians living on the island, which they called Borinquén. There was little gold to plunder, and those first

Spaniards quickly moved on. Their first settlement was established at Caparra in 1509,
but was soon abandoned to the mosquitoes.
The Spaniards moved out of the marshes to
the promontory beside the great bay and began to build a town they called San Juan
Bautista, for St. John the Baptist, who remains the island's patron saint. They built
from memory, combining the Islamic clarity
and the proportions of Andalusia with houses
glimpsed in the Canary Islands before the
passage across the fierce Atlantic. They used
brick and the ax-breaking hardwood called
ausubo as well as iron forged in their own
shops. They built the place to last.

The city they made evolved over centuries, of
course, and even today the urban archaeolo-
gists of the Institute of Puerto Rican Culture
are trying to chart its transformations. This
is no simple task. Although minibuses now
move through the old town, and taxis can
take you to some key points (other streets are
blocked to cars), the best way to see San Juan
is on foot.

As you walk the streets, you tread upon blue-
slag bricks called *adoquines*. Some guides insist they were originally ballast in the sailing
ships of the 17th and 18th centuries, dumped
here as the ships took on cargoes of sugar and
tobacco for the markets of Europe; others tell
you they arrived in San Juan from England as
late as 1890. But they feel as if they had been
here from the beginning, glistening with
spring rain, perfect complements to the suf-
fused yellow light.

Ni modo; it doesn't matter. They are part of
San Juan forever. So is the feeling that here
you might be safe. Three fortresses guard
the city: La Fortaleza–the oldest executive
mansion in the hemisphere, now occupied by
the island's governor—overlooking the bay
on the southwest of the promontory; San

Cristóbal, to the right as you enter the old town from the hotels of the Condado; the magnificent El Morro on the tip, its cannon pointing northwest into the Atlantic. Walls surround the city, linking the three great fortresses, walls of stone.

These walls and forts were not empty adornment; they were, like most things of beauty, a necessity. San Juan was established in an age of international gangsterism, and, since it was usually the last stop for Spanish galleons groaning with the loot of Mexico and Peru, hijackers saw it as an obvious target. Today, you can walk along the edge of El Morro, on walls that are 20 feet thick and rise 140 feet above the sea, and imagine what it was like when unfriendly sails on the horizon could mean death and destruction.

The fort was completed in 1589 by a team of military engineers headed by Juan Bautista Antonelli. The noted English gangster, Francis Drake, appeared in 1595 and was battered by the fort's six levels of cannons, along with fire from the smaller guns of La Fortaleza. Ten of Drake's ships were sunk, and more than 400 sailors were sent to the bottom of the harbor. But, three years later, another English hood, the Earl of Cumberland, arrived and came upon the city from the land side with a force of a thousand soldiers. He occupied San Juan, looted it, and then was forced to abandon it as more than 400 of his men perished from disease. El Morro never was captured again, although the Dutch tried in 1625, managing to burn a number of buildings in San Juan, including the finest private library then in existence in the New World. American naval gunners blasted away at the walls in 1898, during the war against Spain that made Puerto Rico an American colony. They never did take the fortress.

Today, you can visit El Morro on foot, with better luck than Cumberland's doomed soldiers. You go through the 27-acre park grounds, where soldiers once drilled and lovers now meet and fathers play ball with their sons. Hugo did its best against the park, damaging some 50 Australian pines that once lined its entrance. The National Park Service subsequently cut them down.

The hurricane also caused minor damage to the fort, but across the centuries it has survived well. Its walls are the color of lions, its arches painted white, and you cross a dry moat to enter the interior. From the ramparts, you can look down upon crashing surf, or you can visit the museum and souvenir shop, or examine the restored lighthouse, or photograph the domed sentry boxes called *garitas*. You can watch the pretty girls. Or you can simply surrender to the sense of time.

In the area of El Morro, I always save an hour to wander through the 19th-century cemetery below the fortress walls; here lie many of the most famous Puerto Rican political leaders, the martyred revolutionaries, some of the old Spanish *peninsulares* (who lived lives of leisure while slaves did the work), and ordinary folk, too; shopkeepers and blacksmiths, shoemakers and chefs, and the artisans and craftsmen who built the town and died at home. Or I visit awhile in La Casa Blanca, the oldest house on the island, built for Ponce de León in 1521. Ponce was a mixture of romantic and conqueror. He dreamed, as they all did in that generation of Spanish adventurers, of gold. In Puerto Rico, he found little of it—certainly nothing on the scale of the great treasures of Mexico. He stayed on for a while as governor, watching the Tainos die of European diseases or flee to the jungled hills or depart down through the islands in great hand-hewn boats.

They were strange, those dark-skinned pagans; they simply would not agree to be slaves. So Ponce de León departed for Florida in search of the Fountain of Youth, almost certainly a fabrication invented by an Indian. Ponce was still searching in Florida when he was killed in a skirmish with Indians much fiercer that the pacific Tainos. His body was first taken to Cuba, then to San Juan, and his bones are now in the Metropolitan Cathedral. But the elegant Casa Blanca remained in the Ponce family until the late 18th century. The town rose around them. Streets were laid out, fountains constructed, churches built. The energy of the first generation of conquistadores waned throughout the vast Spanish empire; adventurers were replaced with clerks and grandees. The family grew rich, was battered by history, and departed after 250 years. A series of Spanish and then American military commanders lived here, strutting around the lovely courtyard and the splashing fountains. The house is now occupied by the Institute for Advanced Studies.

As an object made by men, a collective work of sculpture, El Castillo de San Cristóbal is, to me, preferable to El Morro. You can walk to it along the city walls, looking down at La Perla, the most picturesque slum under the American flag (it was described in detail in anthropologist Oscar Lewis' book *La Vida*). In ordinary times, the green-tar-paper roofs of La Perla, and the flags of the island's political parties, stand precariously between the city walls and the sea. But Hugo blew the flags into eternity, ripped the tar paper from many rooftops, and battered some of the frailer structures. This was nothing new. Houses have been washed away by storms in the past, but the people of La Perla always

come back and build again. Now, children run
in the streets and winos flake out against the
sides of houses. Years ago, I used to visit
friends down here, but they don't live in La
Perla anymore. And in the age of crack co-
caine I no longer have the courage to wander
its improvised streets.

Instead, I go to San Cristóbal, designed by
two of those Irishmen known as the "wild
geese"—the men and women who scattered
around the world after the English conquest
of their home island. Two who came to Puerto
Rico were, Alejandro O'Reilly and Thomas
O'Daly, and, in the employ of the Spanish
Army, they designed a fort laced with tunnels, secret traps, blind walls, gates, and
pickets. The intention was to protect San
Juan from land invasions, similar to Cumberland's. There are forts within forts here, like
watertight compartments in ships. An invad-
er might take part of the fortress, but would
pay a bloody and ferocious price to take it all.

I love the view from the ramparts of this fort,
looking east toward the beaches and gigantic
clouds that gather above the rain forest of the
mountain called El Yunque. I like to think of
O'Reilly and O'Daly, with their noses peel-
ing, standing in the great blinding light of the
summer sun, far from home, on a promontory
cooled by the trade winds, speaking in Irish
about one final go with the hated English.

Within the city's walls, there are streets that
resemble those of New Orleans, with elabo-
rately scrolled iron, balconies attached to
three-story houses that loom imperiously
above their smaller neighbors. Most were
built in the 17th and 18th centuries by the hi-
dalgos who grew rich from tobacco, sugar,
and horses. The ceiling beams and front
doors are cut from the ausubo tree, so hard
that is has been known to make restoration
workers cry. The austere walls are human-

ized by the bright colors of the Caribbean: lime green, aqua, cerulean blue, rose, and, of course, those warm ochres and yellows. In other places, such colors might seem garish; here, they are as natural and permanent as the sky and the sea.

But some things do change. When I first came to San Juan, there was always music coming from those scrolled balconies, through the open doors of apartments: The Trio Los Panchos and Tito Rodriguez, Agustín Lara and Lucho Gatica, music romantic and bittersweet, occasionally punctuated by the tougher rhythms of mambo. There is less music in the streets now because prosperity has brought air conditioning to Viejo San Juan, and, as everywhere in the world, air conditioning closes windows and doors.

But if there is less to hear, there is still much to see. You gaze into patios that are like snatches of Seville; small fountains, bird cages, polished-iron implements, flowers. All manner of flowers grow in elaborate terracotta pots: philodendron, orchids, the yellowing vines called canarios, bougainvillea spilling from balconies, and hibiscus—mounds, garlands, bowers of hibiscus. There is an occasional flamboyant tree, with its scarlet flowers, imprisoned in its city garden; or a flowering oleander or frangipani preening for the hibiscus. You see palm trees, too, those immigrants from Africa, with terns rattling in the fronds.

Most windows are shuttered, the mute houses implying that in the great Spanish centuries, the densest human life was lived behind them. The town was too small then, too bourgeois, too formal for public melodramas.

Today, life is more public. San Juan is not a museum, and as you wander the streets you can see old men playing dominoes in small, shaded squares, middle-aged women shopping in the boutiques or stopping in La Bombonera on Calle San Francisco for splendid coffee and oversweet pastries, and young people everywhere. I'm not much of a shopper; I'd rather look and imagine than own. So I ignore the shops and follow no set route on my wanderings through Viejo San Juan. I want to be reassured and surprised.

I always go to the Cristo Chapel on the city walls overlooking the harbor. Almost always it is as I saw it last, closed off by an iron gate, four potted palms within its small interior, the masonry peeled off parts of the walls to reveal the thin brick of the past. The palms were demolished by Hugo; they will be replaced. One need not share the belief that inspired the chapel to be charmed by its proportions and modesty. As always, the little park beside it is filled with children and pigeons. A plaque tells me that the chapel was built between 1753 and 1780 and that "legend traces its origin to a miraculous happening at the site." It doesn't describe the miracle, but it is said that in 1753 a rider in a holy festival made a mistake, plunged over the wall into the sea, and lived. Not exactly a major miracle, I suppose, but good enough to get the chapel built. The plaque bears the seal of Lions International.

As in most Latin countries, the sacred and the profane, are at war here. All over Old San Juan, there are dozens of little bars. On the corner of San Sebastián and San Justo there is a bar called Aquí Se Puede, which means "here you can," and in its cool, dark interior the name seems more an act of reporting than of enticement.

A few blocks away is the Church of San José —spare, controlled, set facing a square out of deChirico. It is the oldest church still in active use in the Americas, built by Dominican friars in the 1530s. But the mood within is of an austere European Catholicism exiled to the tropics. Plain song comes from a hidden sound system. Natural light falls from openings in the cupolas of side chapels. The wooden pews are severe. The stations of the cross, with their ancient tale of sacrifice and pain, are bichromes of blue and white. Most afternoons, there is an eerie silence in the place, perhaps for good reason; archives suggest that as many as four thousand people—including most of the descendants of Ponce de León—might be buried beneath the tile floors.

On hot days, I used to stop for a while in the Plaza de Armas, to sit under the shade trees and talk to the taxi drivers and lounging cops and gold-toothed old men. They all told fabulous lies, and, across the street, vendors sold flowers under the arches of City Hall. There were department stores on the harbor side and pretty girls everywhere. The stores and pretty girls remain; all the rest is changed.

In 1988, a mayor named Balthasar Corrado del Rió insisted on remodeling the plaza his way. Citizens protested, but he went ahead anyway—the shade trees were chain sawed at four in the morning. A cheap phone kiosk was erected. And now the Plaza de Armas is a bald, bright plain.

Now, if it's a hot day, I walk across the plaza to the corner of the New York Department Store, toward the harbor along Calle San José. I go into The Bookstore, which is air conditioned and has a fine selection of books in English, along with the latest volumes from Mexico, Buenos Aires, and Barcelona, and the works of such fine Puerto Rican writers as Pedro Juan Soto, Luis Rafael Sanchez, and Rene Marquez. Here I can also pick up a copy of *The New York Times*. Then I

go next door into the Café de Los Amigos for
the best coffee in the old town. A sign sets out
one of the rules: *No Discuta Politica Aquí.*

There are other plazas, churches, and museums, of course; your legs will carry you to all
of them, or, in revolt, will persuade you to see
them at some later date. But the people are as
important as the buildings. On Saturday
nights, the young people of the other San
Juan show up to party in Viejo San Juan;
handsome young men in the pretty-boy
guapo style—hair slicked wearing New
York fashions, playing out roles that they
haven't earned; the young women, voluptuous, made up to look like Madonna or one of
the stars of Spanish television, their bodies
bursting from tight skirts, T-shirts, and
blouses.

There is something sad about them, as they
preen for each other in the ancient rituals.
They seem like so many tropical flowers
blooming briefly before the swift move into
adulthood. On these weekend evenings, they
stand outside the Daiquiri Factory on Calle
San Francisco, or Joseph's Café next door,
some of them drinking and dancing inside
while MTV plays on giant screens. They come
to Viejo San Juan from the modern city of
plastic and cement, as if subconsciously seeking to discover who they are by temporarily
inhabiting the places from which their families came.

The perfumed rituals are enacted amidst the
colliding symbols of the island's general cultural schizophrenia: Kentucky Fried Chick-
en, Burger King, and McDonald's, along with
El Convento and the Plaza Salvador Brau,
where there is a statue of a man named
Patricio Rijos, who was known in life as
"Toribio, King of the Guiro." The guiro is a
grooved gourd played as a rhythm instru-

ment with a wire fork. It is never seen on MTV.

And as the children of those San Juan nights careen away to various appointments, the music gradually stops, doors are shuttered, the traffic departs. At 104 Calle Fortaleza, on one such evening, I stopped to look at a marble plaque that identified the building as: "THE HOUSE WHERE IN 1963 THE PIÑA COLADA WAS CREATED BY DON RAMÓN PORTA MINGOT." It was now a perfume shop called Barrachina. I smiled, thinking that in Viejo San Juan, all of the important things are remembered, when a small, wiry man came up to me.

"*Es una mentira,*" he said. "It's a lie. It was the bar of the Caribe Hilton, 1958."

Without another word, he walked off on unsteady legs, humming an old song. I went back to the hotel, to dream of yellow light.

3 Exploring Puerto Rico

Introduction

*by Honey
Naylor*

No city in the Caribbean is as steeped in Spanish tradition as Puerto Rico's Old San Juan. Old San Juan's attractions are myriad: restored 16th-century buildings, museums, art galleries, bookstores, 200-year-old houses with balustraded balconies of filigreed wrought iron overlooking quaint, narrow, cobblestone streets. This Spanish tradition also spills over into the island's countryside, from its festivals celebrated in honor of various patron saints in the little towns, to the paradors, those homey, inexpensive inns whose concept originated in Spain.

Puerto Rico has, in San Juan's sophisticated Condado and Isla Verde areas, glittering hotels, flashy, Las Vegas–style shows, casinos, and frenetic discos. It has the ambience of the Old World in the seven-square-block area of the old city and in its quiet colonial towns. Out in the countryside lie its natural attractions—the extraordinary, 28,000-acre Caribbean National Forest, more familiarly known as the El Yunque rain forest, with its 100-foot-high trees, more than 200 species of them, and its dramatic mountain ranges; there are forest reserves with trails to satisfy the most dedicated hiker, vast caves to tempt spelunkers, coffee plantations, old sugar mills, and hundreds of beaches.

Puerto Rico, 110 miles long and 35 miles wide, was populated by several tribes of Indians when Columbus landed on the island on his second voyage in 1493. In 1508, Juan Ponce de Léon, the frustrated searcher of the Fountain of Youth, established a settlement on the island and became its first governor, and in 1521, founded Old San Juan. For three centuries, the Dutch and the English tried unsuccessfully to wrest the island from Spain. In 1897, Spain granted the island dominion status. Two years later, Spain ceded the island to the United States, and in 1917 Puerto Ricans became U.S. citizens, part of the Commonwealth.

And so, if you're a U.S. citizen, you need neither passport nor visa when you land at the bustling Luis Muñoz Marín Airport, outside San Juan.

Puerto Rico

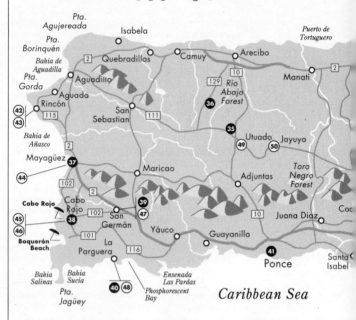

ATLANTIC OCEAN

Pta.
Agujereada
Pta.
Borinquén
Bahia de
Aguadilla
Pta.
Gorda
Rincón
Bahia de
Añasco
Mayagüez
Cabo Rojo
Boquerón
Beach
Bahia
Salinas
Bahia
Sucia
Pta.
Jagüey

Isabela
Quebradillas
Aguadilla
Aguada
San
Sebastian
Maricao
Cabo
Rojo
San
Germán
La
Parguera
Ensenada
Las Pardas
Phosphorescent
Bay

Camuy
Arecibo
Río
Abajo
Forest
Utuado
Jayuya
Adjuntas
Yáuco
Guayanilla
Ponce

Puerto de
Tortuguero
Manati
Toro
Negro
Forest
Juana Diaz
Santa
Isabel

Caribbean Sea

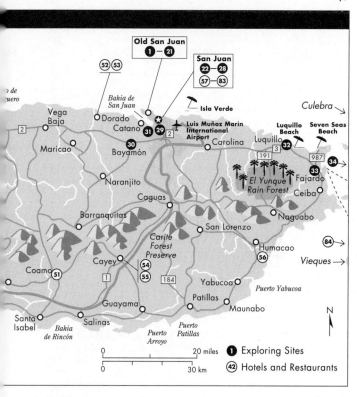

You don't have to clear customs, and you don't have to explain yourself to an immigration official. English is widely spoken, though the official language is Spanish.

Puerto Rico also boasts hundreds of beaches with every imaginable water sport available, acres of golf courses and miles of tennis courts, and small colonial towns where you can quietly savor the Spanish flavor. If it's festivals you seek, every town honors its individual patron saint with an annual festival, which is usually held in the central plaza, and can last from one to 10 days. In San Juan, *LeLoLai* is a year-round festival celebrating Puerto Rican dance and folklore, with changing programs presented in major San Juan hotels. Having seen every sight on the island, you can then do further exploring on the offshore islands of Culebra, Vieques, Icacos, and Mona, where more aquatic activities, such as snorkeling and scuba diving, prevail.

Old San Juan

Numbers in the margin correspond with points of interest on the Old San Juan map.

① Old San Juan, the original city founded in 1521, contains authentic and carefully preserved examples of 16th- and 17th-century Spanish colonial architecture, some of the best in the New World. More than 400 buildings have been beautifully restored. Graceful wrought-iron balconies, decorated with lush green hanging plants, extend over narrow streets paved with blue-gray stones (*adequines,* originally used as ballast for Spanish ships). The old city is partially enclosed by the old walls, dating from 1630, that once completely surrounded it. Designated a U.S. National Historic Zone in 1950, Old San Juan is chockablock with shops, open-air cafés, private homes, tree-shaded squares, monuments, plaques, pigeons, and people. The traffic is awful. Get an overview of the inner city on a morning's stroll (bearing in mind that "stroll" includes some steep climbs). However, if you plan to immerse yourself in history, or to shop, you'll need two or three days.

Old San Juan

ATLANTIC OCEAN

N

Del Morro

Calle de Norzagaray

Virtud San Sebastian
Sol
Luna O'Donnell
Muñoz Rivera

Cruz
San
Del San José
Los Monjas
San Francisco
Ponce de Léon
Fortaleza
Paseo de Covadonga
Cristo
José
Tetuán Recinto
Princesa
Sur
Marina
Del Muelle
Arsenal

Bahia de San Juan

```
0        550 yards
0        500 meters
```

Casa Blanca, **8**
Casa del Libro, **13**
City Hall, **17**
Cristo Chapel, **12**
Dominican Convent (Institute of Puerto Rican Culture), **7**

Fine Arts Museum, **14**
La Casa de los Contrafuertes, **4**
La Fortaleza, **11**
La Intendencia, **16**
Old San Juan, **1**

Pablo Casals Museum, **5**
Plaza de Armas, **15**
Plaza de Colón, **18**
Plazuela de la Rogativa, **10**
Port, **21**
San Cristóbal, **20**
San Felipe del Morro, **2**

San José Church, **6**
San Juan Cathedral, **9**
San Juan Museum of Arts and History, **3**
Tapia Theater, **19**

El Morro and Fort San Cristóbal are described in our walking tour: You may want to set aside extra time to see them, especially if you're an aficionado of military history. UNESCO has designated each fortress a World Heritage Site; each is also a National Historic Site. Both are looked after by the National Park Service; you can take one of their tours or wander around on your own.

❷ Sitting on a rocky promontory on the northwestern tip of the old city is **San Felipe del Morro** ("El Morro"), a fortress built by the Spaniards between 1540 and 1783. Rising 140 feet above the sea, the massive six-level fortress covers enough territory to accommodate a nine-hole golf course. It is a labyrinth of dungeons, ramps and barracks, turrets, towers, and tunnels. Built to protect the port, El Morro has a commanding view of the harbor. Its small, air-conditioned museum traces the history of the fortress. *Calle Norzagaray, tel. 809/724–1974. Admission: $1 adults, children free. Open daily 8–6:15.*

❸ San José Plaza is two short blocks from the entrance to El Morro, but for the moment we'll bypass it and head for the **San Juan Museum of Arts and History,** which is a block east of the tour's path but a must. A bustling marketplace in 1850, this handsome building is now a modern cultural center that houses exhibits of Puerto Rican art. Multi-image audiovisual shows present the history of the island; concerts and other cultural events take place in the huge courtyard. *Calle Norzagaray, at the corner of Calle MacArthur, tel. 809/724–1875. Donation requested: $1 adults, 50¢ children. Open Tues.–Sat. 8–noon and 1–4. Audiovisual shows weekdays 11 AM and 1:15 PM.*

❹ Turn back west toward San José Plaza to **La Casa de los Contrafuertes,** on Calle San Sebastián. This building is also known as the Buttress House because wide exterior buttresses support the wall next to the plaza. The house is one of the oldest remaining private residences in Old San Juan. Inside is the Pharmacy Museum, a re-creation of an 18th-century apothecary shop. The building was closed for renovation at press time. *101 Calle San Sebastián, Plaza de*

*San José, tel. 809/724–5949. Admission free.
Open Wed.–Sun. 9–noon and 1–4.*

⑤ The **Pablo Casals Museum,** a bit farther down
the block, contains memorabilia of the famed
cellist, who made his home in Puerto Rico for
the last 20 years of his life. The museum holds
manuscripts, photographs, and his favorite cel-
los, in addition to recordings and videotapes of
Casals Festival concerts (the latter shown on re-
quest). *101 Calle San Sebastián, Plaza de San
José, tel. 809/723–9185. Admission free. Open
Tues.–Sat. 9:30–5:30; Sun. 1–5; closed Mon.*

In the center of the plaza, next to the museum, is
⑥ the **San José Church.** With its series of vaulted
ceilings, it is a splendid example of 16th-century
Spanish Gothic architecture. The church, which
is one of the oldest Christian houses of worship
in the Western Hemisphere, was built in 1532
under the supervision of the Dominican friars.
The body of Ponce de León, the Spanish explorer who came to the New World seeking the
Fountain of Youth, was buried here for almost
three centuries before being removed in 1913
and placed in the cathedral. *Calle San Sebastián, tel. 809/725–7501. Admission free. Open
Mon.–Sat. 8:30–4; Sun. noon mass.*

⑦ Next door is the **Dominican Convent (Institute
of Puerto Rican Culture).** Built by Dominican
friars in 1523, the convent often served as a shel-
ter during Carib Indian attacks in the past and,
more recently, as headquarters for the Antilles
command of the U.S. Army. Now home to the
Institute of Puerto Rican Culture, the beautifully restored building contains an ornate 18th-
century altar, religious manuscripts, artifacts,
and art. Classical concerts are occasionally held
here. *98 Calle Norzagaray, tel. 809/724–0700.
Admission free. Chapel museum open Wed.–
Sun. 9–noon and 1–4. Popular Arts Museum
open Mon.–Sat. 9:15–4:15.*

From San José Plaza walk west on Calle
⑧ Beneficencia to **Casa Blanca.** The original structure on this site, not far from the ramparts of El
Morro, was a frame house built in 1521 as a home
for Ponce de León. But Ponce de León died in
Cuba, never having lived in the house, and it was
virtually destroyed by a hurricane in 1523, after

which Ponce de León's son-in-law had the present masonry house built. His descendants occupied it for 250 years. From the end of the Spanish-American War in 1898 to 1966, it was the home of the U.S. Army commander in Puerto Rico. It is now a museum showcasing aspects of 16th- and 17th-century Puerto Rican family life. Guided tours are conducted Tuesday–Saturday. *1 Calle San Sebastián, tel. 809/724–4102. Admission free. Open Tues.–Sat. 9–noon and 1–4:30.*

❾ San Juan Cathedral. This great Catholic shrine of Puerto Rico had humble beginnings in the early 1520s as a thatch-topped wood structure. Hurricane winds tore off the thatch and destroyed the church. It was reconstructed in 1540, when the graceful circular staircase and vaulted ceilings were added, but most of the work on the church was done in the 19th century. The remains of Ponce de León are in a marble tomb near the transept. *153 Calle Cristo. Open daily 6:30–5.*

Time Out Stop in at **María's** (204 Calle Cristo, no phone) for a papaya freeze, a chocolate frost, or a pitcher of Mexican sangría. Enchiladas and tacos are also served.

Across the street from the cathedral you'll see the Ramada Gran Hotel El Convento, which was a Carmelite convent more than 300 years ago. Go west alongside the hotel on Caleta de las **❿** Monjas toward the city wall to the **Plazuela de la Rogativa.** In the little plaza, statues of a bishop and three women commemorate a legend, according to which the British, while laying siege to the city in 1797, mistook the flaming torches of a religious procession *(rogativa)* for Spanish reinforcements and beat a hasty retreat. The monument was donated to the city in 1971 on its 450th anniversary.

One block south on Calle Recinto Oeste you'll **⓫** come to **La Fortaleza,** which sits on a hill overlooking the harbor. La Fortaleza, the Western Hemisphere's oldest executive mansion in continuous use, home of 170 governors and official residence of the present governor of Puerto Rico, was built as a fortress. The original primitive structure, built in 1540, has seen numerous changes over a period of three centuries, resulting in the present collection of marble and mahogany, medieval towers, and stained-glass galleries. Guided tours are conducted every hour on the hour in English, on the half hour in Spanish. *Tel. 809/721-7000. Admission free. Open weekdays 9-4.*

⑫ At the southern end of Cristo Street is **Cristo Chapel.** According to legend, in 1753 a young horseman, carried away during festivities in honor of the patron saint, raced down the street and plunged over the steep precipice. A witness to the tragedy promised to build a chapel if the young man's life could be saved. The man lived. Inside is a small silver altar, dedicated to the Christ of Miracles. *Open Tues. 10-4 and on most Catholic holidays.*

⑬ Across the street from the chapel, the 18th-century **Casa del Libro** has exhibits devoted to books and bookbinding. The museum's 5,000 books include rare volumes dating back 2,000 years; more than 200 of these books—40 of which were produced in Spain—were printed before the 16th century. *255 Calle Cristo, tel. 809/723-0354. Admission free. Open weekdays (except holidays) 11-4:30.*

⑭ Next door, the **Fine Arts Museum,** in a lovely colonial building, occasionally presents special exhibits. The museum usually holds the Institute of Puerto Rican Culture's collection of paintings and sculptures, but those pieces have been temporarily removed. *253 Calle Cristo, tel. 809/724-5949. Admission free. Open 9-noon and 1-4:30.*

⑮ Follow the wall east one block and head north on Calle San José two short blocks to **Plaza de Armas,** the original main square of Old San Juan. The plaza, bordered by Calles San Francisco, Fortaleza, San José, and Cruz, has a lovely fountain with statues representing the four seasons.

⑯ West of the square stands **La Intendencia,** a handsome three-story neoclassical building. From 1851 to 1898, it was home to the Spanish Treasury. Recently restored, it is now the headquarters of Puerto Rico's State Department.

Calle San José, at the corner of Calle San Francisco, tel. 809/722–2121. Admission free. Open weekdays 8–noon and 1–4:30.

17 On the north side of the plaza is **City Hall,** called the *Alcaldía.* Built between 1604 and 1789, the alcaldía was fashioned after Madrid's city hall, with arcades, towers, balconies, and a lovely inner courtyard. A tourist information center and an art gallery are on the first floor. *Tel. 809/724–7171. Open weekdays 8–4.*

Time Out   **La Bombonera** (259 Calle San Francisco, no phone), established in 1903, is known for its strong Puerto Rican coffee and *Mallorca*—a Spanish pastry made of light dough, toasted, buttered, and sprinkled with powdered sugar.

18 Four blocks east on the pedestrian mall of Calle Fortaleza you'll find **Plaza de Colón,** a bustling square with a statue of Christopher Columbus atop a high pedestal. Originally called St. James Square, it was renamed in honor of Columbus on the 400th anniversary of the discovery of Puerto Rico. Bronze plaques in the base of the statue relate various episodes in the life of the great explorer. On the north side of the plaza is a terminal for buses to and from San Juan.

19 South of Plaza de Colón is the magnificent **Tapia Theater** (Calle Fortaleza at Plaza de Colón, tel. 809/722–0407), named after the famed Puerto Rican playwright Alejandro Tapia y Riviera. Built in 1832, remodeled in 1949 and again in 1987, the municipal theater is the site of ballets, plays, and operettas. Stop by the box office to see what's showing and if you can get tickets.

20 Walk two blocks north from Plaza de Colón to Calle Sol and turn right. Another block will take you to **San Cristóbal,** the 18th-century fortress that guarded the city from land attacks. Even larger than El Morro, San Cristóbal was known as the Gibraltar of the West Indies. *Tel. 809/724–1974. Admission free. Open daily 8–6:15.*

21 Stroll from Plaza de Colón down to the **Port,** where the esplanade is spruced up with flowers, trees, and street lamps. Across from Pier 3, where the cruise ships dock, local artisans display their wares at the Plazoleta del Puerto. At the marina, pay 20¢ and board a ferry for a round-trip ride to Catano.

New San Juan

Numbers in the margin correspond with points of interest on the San Juan map.

You'll need to resort to taxis, buses, públicos, or a rental car to reach the points of interest in **22** **"new" San Juan.**

Avenida Muñoz Rivera, Avenida Ponce de León, and Avenida Fernández Juncos are the main thoroughfares that cross Puerta de Tierra, just east of Old San Juan, to the business and tourist districts of Santurce, Condado, and Isla Verde.

23 In Puerta de Tierra is Puerto Rico's **Capitol,** a white marble building that dates from the 1920s. The grand rotunda, with mosaics and friezes, was completed a few years ago. The seat of the island's bicameral legislature, the Capitol contains Puerto Rico's Constitution and is flanked by the modern buildings of the Senate and the House of Representatives. There are spectacular views from the observation plaza on the sea side of the Capitol. Pick up an informative booklet about the building from the House Secretariat on the second floor. Guided tours are by appointment only. *Avenida Ponce de León, tel. 809/721–7305 or 721–7310. Admission free. Open weekdays 8:30–5.*

24 At the eastern tip of Puerta de Tierra, behind the splashy Caribe Hilton, the tiny **Fort San Jeronimo** is perched over the Atlantic like an afterthought. Added to San Juan's fortifications in the late 18th century, the structure barely survived the British attack of 1797. Restored in 1983 by the Institute of Puerto Rican Culture, it is now a military museum with displays of weapons, uniforms, and maps. *Tel. 809/724–5949. Admission free. Open Wed.–Sun. 9:30–noon and 1:30–4:30.*

Dos Hermanos Bridge connects Puerta de Tierra with Miramar, Condado, and Isla Grande. Isla Grande Airport, from which you can take short hops, is on the bay side of the bridge.

San Juan Exploring, Dining, and Lodging

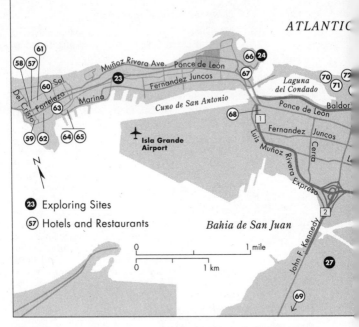

ATLANTIC

23 Exploring Sites

57 Hotels and Restaurants

Bahia de San Juan

Exploring

Capitol, **23**

Fine Arts Center, **26**

Fort San Jeronimo, **24**

Muñoz Marín Park, **27**

New San Juan, **22**

Santurce, **25**

University of Puerto Rico, **28**

Dining

Amadeus, **60**

Ambrosia, **58**

Augusto's, **68**

Cafeteria España, **82**

The Chart House, **77**

Che's, **81**

Dar Tiffany, **80**

El Nuevo Cafe San Juan, **62**

El Paso, **69**

El Patio del Convento, **57**

Il Giardino, **76**

Kasalta Bakery, Inc., **79**

L.K. Sweeney & Son, Ltd., **70**

La Chaumiere, **63**

La Compostela, **75**

La Reina de España, **73**

La Rotisserie, **66**

La Zaragozana, **61**

Santiago, **64**

Scotch & Sirloin, **71**

Via Appia's Italian Deli, **78**

Yukjyu, **65**

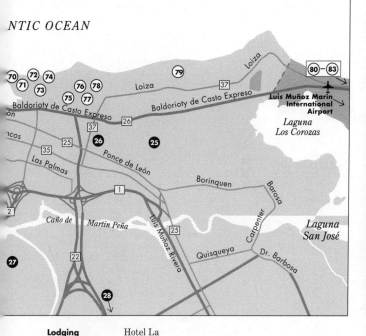

Lodging

Caribe Hilton International, **66**

Condado Beach Hotel, **72**

Condado Plaza Hotel & Casino, **70**

El San Juan Hotel and Casino, **80**

Excelsior, **68**

Hotel La Concha, **74**

Radisson Normandie Hotel, **67**

Ramada Gran Hotel El Convento, **59**

Sands Hotel and Casino, **83**

On the other side of the bridge, the Condado Lagoon is bordered by Avenida Ashford, which threads past the high-rise Condado hotels and El Centro Convention Center, and Avenida Baldorioty de Castro, which barrels all the way east to the airport and beyond. Due south of the lagoon is Miramar, a primarily residential area with fashionable, turn-of-the-century homes and a cluster of hotels and restaurants.

㉕ Santurce, which lies between Miramar on the west and the San José Lagoon on the east, is a busy mixture of shops, markets, and offices. Internationally acclaimed performers appear at **㉖** the **Fine Arts Center.** This completely modern facility, the largest of its kind in the Caribbean, has a full schedule of concerts, plays, and operas. *Centro de Bellas Artes, corner of De Diego Ave. and Ponce de León St., tel. 809/724-4751.*

South of Santurce is the "Golden Mile"—Hato Rey, the city's bustling new financial hub. Isla Verde, with its glittering beachfront hotels, casinos, discos, and public beach, is to the east, near the airport.

Time Out **Pescadería Atlántica** (81 Loiza St., tel. 809/726-6654) is a combination seafood restaurant and retail store. Stop in for a cool drink at the bar and a side dish of calamares, lightly breaded squid in a hot, spicy sauce.

Northeast of Isla Verde, Boca de Cangrejos sits between the Atlantic and Torrecilla Lagoon—a great spot for fishing and snorkeling. This is the point of embarkation for the 30-passenger launch, *La Paseadora*, which tours the coast, the mangrove swamp, and the bird sanctuary at Torrecilla Lagoon.

Southeast of Miramar, Avenida Muñoz Rivera skirts along the northern side of **San Juan Central Park,** a convenient place for jogging, tennis, and calisthenics. The mangrove-bordered park was built for the 1979 Pan-American Games. *Cerra St. exit on Rte. 2, tel. 809/722-1646. Admission free. Open Tues.–Sat. 8–10, Mon. 2–10, Sun. 10–6.*

Las Américas Expressway, heading south, goes by Plaza Las Américas, the largest shopping mall in the Caribbean, and takes you to the new **Muñoz Marín Park,** an idyllic tree-shaded spot dotted with gardens, lakes, playgrounds, and picnic areas. Cable cars connect the park with the parking area. *Next to Las Américas Expwy., west on Piñero Ave., tel. 809/763–0568. Admission free; parking $1 per vehicle. Open Tues.–Fri., 9–6, weekends 8:30–6; closed Mon.*

Río Piedras, a southern suburb of San Juan, is home to the **University of Puerto Rico,** located between Ponce de León Avenue and Barbosa Avenue. The university's campus is one of two sites for performances of the Puerto Rico Symphony Orchestra. Theatrical productions and other concerts are also scheduled here throughout the year. The University Museum has permanent archaeological and historical exhibits, and occasionally mounts special art displays. *Next to the university main entrance on Ponce de León Ave., tel. 809/764–0000, ext. 2452 or 2456. Open weekdays 9–9, weekends 9–3.*

The university's main attraction is the **Botanical Garden,** a lush garden with more than 200 species of tropical and subtropical vegetation. Footpaths through the thick forests lead to a graceful lotus lagoon, a bamboo promenade, an orchid garden, and a palm garden. *Intersection of Rtes. 1 and 847 at the entrance to Barrio Venezuela, tel. 809/766–0740. Admission free. Open Tues.–Sun. 9–4:30; when Mon. is a holiday, it is open Mon. and closed Tues.*

San Juan Environs

Numbers in the margin correspond with points of interest on the Puerto Rico map.

From San Juan, follow Route 2 west toward Bayamón and you'll spot the **Caparra Ruins,** where, in 1508, Ponce de León established the island's first settlement. The ruins are that of an ancient fort. Its small **Museum of the Conquest and Colonization of Puerto Rico** contains historical documents, exhibits, and excavated artifacts. (You can see the museum's contents in less time than it takes to say the name.) *Km 6.6 on Rte. 2, tel. 809/781–4795. Admission free. Open weekdays 9–5, weekends and holidays 10–6.*

30 Continue on Route 2 to **Bayamón.** In the Central Park, across from Bayamón's city hall, there are some historical buildings and a 1934 sugarcane train that runs through the park (open daily 8 AM–10 PM). On the plaza, in the city's historic district, stands the 18th-century Catholic church of Santa Cruz, and the old neoclassical city hall, which now houses the **Francisco Oller Art and History Museum** (open Tues.–Sat. 9–4).

31 Along Route 5 from Bayamón to Catano, you'll see the **Barrilito Rum Plant.** On the grounds is a 200-year-old plantation home and a 150-year-old windmill, which is listed in the National Register of Historic Places.

The **Bacardi Rum Plant,** along the bay, conducts 45-minute tours of the bottling plant, museum, and distillery, which has the capacity to produce 100,000 gallons of rum a day. (Yes, you'll be offered a sample.) *Km 2.6 on Rte. 888, tel. 809/788-1500. Admission free. Tours Mon.–Sat. 9:30–3:30; closed Sun.*

Out on the Island

Puerto Rico's 3,500 square miles is a lot of land to explore. While it is possible to get from town to town via público, we don't recommend traveling that way unless your Spanish is good and you know exactly where you're going. The public cars stop in each town's main square, leaving you on your own to reach the beaches, restaurants, paradors, and sightseeing attractions. You'll do much better if you rent a car. Most of the island's roads are excellent. However, there is a tangled web of roads through the mountains, and they are not always well marked. Get a good road map.

East and South 32 Our first excursion out on the island will take us east, down the coast to the south, and back up to San Juan. The first leg of the trip—to **Luquillo Beach** and the nearby **El Yunque rain forest**— can easily be done in a day. (There'll be heavy traffic and a crowded beach on weekends, when it seems as if the whole world heads for Luquillo.) The full itinerary will take two to three days, depending upon how long you loll on the beach and linger over the mountain scenery.

To take full advantage of the 28,000-acre El Yunque rain forest, go with a tour. Dozens of trails lead through the thick jungle (it sheltered the Carib Indians for 200 years), and the tour guides take you to the best observation points. Some of the trails are slippery, and there are occasional washouts.

However, if you'd like to drive there yourself, take Route 3 east from San Juan and turn right (south) on Route 191, about 25 miles from the city. The **Sierra Palm Visitor Center** is on Route 191, Km 11.6 (open daily 9:30–5). Nature talks and programs at the center are by appointment only—another good reason to go with a tour group.

El Yunque, named after the good Indian spirit Yuquiyu, is in the Luquillo Mountain Range. The rain forest is verdant with feathery ferns, thick ropelike vines, white tuberoses and ginger, miniature orchids, and some 240 different species of trees. More than 100 billion gallons of rainwater falls on it annually. Rain-battered, wind-ravaged dwarf vegetation clings to the top peaks. (El Toro, the highest peak in the forest, is 3,532 feet.) El Yunque is also a bird sanctuary and is the base of the rare Puerto Rican parrot. Millions of tiny, inch-long tree frogs *(coquis)* can be heard singing (or squawking, depending on your sensibilities). *For further information call the Catalina Field Office, tel. 809/887–2875 or 809/766–5335; or write Caribbean National Forest, Box B, Palmer, PR 00721.*

To reach Luquillo Beach, take Route 191 back to Route 3 and continue east 5 miles to Km 35.4. One of the island's best and most popular beaches, Luquillo was once a flourishing coconut plantation. Coral reefs protect its calm, pristine lagoon, making it an ideal place for a swim. The entrance fee is 25¢, parking is $1, and there are lockers, showers, and changing rooms *(see* Beaches in Chapter 4: Sports, Fitness, Beaches).

If you want to continue exploring, get back on
33 Route 3 and drive 5 miles to **Fajardo,** a major fishing and sailing center with thousands of boats tied up to its three large marinas. Boats can be rented or chartered here, and the *Spread*

Eagle catamaran can take you out for a full day of snorkeling, swimming, and sunning *(see* Participant Sports in Chapter 4: Sports, Fitness, Beaches). Fajardo is also the embarkation point for ferries to the offshore islands of Culebra (a $2.25 fare) and Vieques ($2). Culebra has lovely white-sand beaches, coral reefs, and a wildlife

34 refuge. In the sleepy town of **Dewey,** on Culebra's southwestern side, check at the Visitor Information Center at city hall (tel. 809/742–3291) about boat rentals. On Vieques, Sun Bay public beach has picnic facilities; Blue Beach is superb for snorkeling; and Mosquito Bay is luminous even on moonless nights. You can stay overnight at the government-sponsored Parador Villa Esperanza (tel. 809/741–8675) on Vieques, which has, among other amenities, its own marina and fleet of sailing ships.

Resume your ramble on Route 3, heading south past the U.S. Naval Base and ride through the sugarcane fields to Humacao. South of Humacao (take Route 906) is the 2,700-acre Palmas del Mar, the island's largest residential resort complex.

Stay on Route 3 through Yabucoa, tucked up in the hills, and Maunabo and Patillas, where you can pick up the routes to take you through the Cayey Mountains. Route 184 north skirts Lake Patillas and cuts smack through the Carite Forest Reserve. Stay on Route 184 until it merges with Route 763. Turn left on Route 763, then right on Route 765 to Route 1, where you'll shoot northward back to San Juan.

Western If you're short of time, drive the 64 miles from
Island San Juan to Ponce in 90 minutes. Take the Las Américas Expressway, which cuts through the splendid mountains of Cordillera Central.

If time is not a major problem, take a three- or four-day tour exploring the western regions of the island. This route covers Aguadilla, Mayagüez, San Germán, and Ponce. There's much to see along the way—caves and coves, karst fields and coffee plantations, mountains and beaches, and even a zoo.

35 Outside Utuado, south of Route 10, is **Caguana Indian Ceremonial Park,** used 800 years ago by the Taino tribes for recreation and worship. Mountains surround a 13-acre site planted with royal palms and guava. According to Spanish historians, the Tainos played a game similar to soccer, and in this park there are 10 courts bordered by cobbled walkways. There are also stone monoliths, some with colorful petroglyphs; a small museum; and a souvenir shop. *Rte. 111, Km 12.3. Admission free. Open daily 8:30–4:30.*

From Utuado, drive west on Route 111 and then north on Route 129 to Km 18.9, where you'll find the **Río Camuy Cave Park,** one of the world's largest cave networks. Guided tours take you on a tram down through dense tropical vegetation to the entrance of the cave, where you continue on foot over underground trails, ramps, and bridges. The caves, sinkholes, and underground rivers are all spectacular (the world's second-largest underground river runs through here), but this trip is not for those with claustrophobia. Be sure to call ahead; the tours allow only a limited number of people. *Rte. 129, Km 18.9, tel. 809/898-3100 or 809/756-5555. Admission: $4 adults, $2.50 children. Open Wed.–Sun. 8–4. Last tour starts at 4.*

Route 111 twists from Utuado to **Aguadilla** on the northwest coast. In this area, somewhere between Aguadilla and Añasco, south of Rincón, Columbus dropped anchor on his second voyage in 1493. Both Aguadilla and **Aguada,** a few miles to the south, claim to have been the spot where his foot first hit ground, and both towns have plaques to commemorate the occasion.

Route 115 from Aguadilla to **Rincón** is one of the island's most scenic drives, through rolling hills dotted with pastel-colored houses. Rincón, perched on a hill, overlooks its beach, which was the site of the World Surfing Championship in 1968. Skilled surfers flock to Rincón during the winter, when the water is rough and challenging.

Pick up Route 2 for the 6-mile drive to **Mayagüez,** Puerto Rico's third-largest city, with a population approaching 100,000. Mayagüez, known for its needlework, has plenty of shops to browse around in. (The Mayagüez

Shopping Mall is one of the island's largest. The lounge of the hilltop Mayagüez Hilton is a popular gathering place for locals and tourists.)

North of town visit the **Mayagüez Zoo,** a 45-acre tropical compound that's home to about 500 animals. In addition to Bengal tigers, reptiles, and birds, including an Andean condor, there's a lake and a children's playground. *Rte. 108 at Barrio Miradero, tel. 809/834–8110. Admission: $1 adults, 50¢ children. Open Tues.–Sun. 9–4:30.*

38 Due south of Mayagüez, via the coastal Route 102, is **Cabo Rojo,** once a pirates' hangout and now a favorite resort area of Puerto Ricans. The area has long stretches of white-sand beaches on the clear, calm Caribbean Sea, as well as many seafood restaurants. There are also several paradores in the region. **Boquerón,** at the end of Route 101, has one of the best beaches on the island, as well as two-room cabins for rent.

61 From Cabo Rojo continue east on Route 102 to **San Germán,** a quiet Old World town that's home to the oldest intact church under the U.S. flag. Built in 1606, Porta Coeli (Gates of Heaven) overlooks one of the town's two plazas (where the townspeople continue the Spanish tradition of promenading at night). The church is now a museum of religious art, housing 18th- and 19th-century paintings and statues. *Tel. 809/892–5845. Admission free. Open Wed.–Sun. 8:30–noon and 1–4:30.*

40 The fishing village of **La Parguera,** an area of simple seafood restaurants, mangrove cays, and small islands, lies south of San Germán at the end of Route 304. This is an excellent scuba-diving area, but the main attraction is **Phosphorescent Bay.** Boats tour the bay, where microscopic dinoflagellates (marine plankton) light up like Christmas trees when disturbed by any kind of movement. The phenomenon can be seen only on moonless nights. Boats leave the pier nightly at 7:30, and the trip costs $4 per person.

From San Germán, Route 2 traverses splendid peaks and valleys; pastel houses cling to the sides of steep green hills. East of Yauco, the

(41) road dips and sweeps right along the Caribbean and into **Ponce.**

Puerto Rico's second city, with a population of about 150,000, has much to explore. You have not seen a firehouse until you've seen the red-and-black-striped **Parque de Bombas,** built in 1883 on the city's central plaza, with its bright yellow firetrucks. Stroll around the plaza, with its perfectly pruned trees, graceful fountains, gardens, and park benches. **Our Lady of Guadalupe Cathedral** would surely dominate the square, were it not for the firehouse. The white-columned **Casa Alcaldía** is the city hall, where you can stop in and pick up information.

Recent efforts to restore the city can be appreciated on the streets surrounding the plaza, where freshly painted houses with wrought-iron balconies, gas lamps, Corinthian columns, and Spanish arches may remind you of New Orleans's French Quarter.

Off the Beaten Track

The Blue Dolphin is a hangout where you can rub elbows with some offbeat locals. Located behind the Empress Oceanfront Hotel at the northern tip of Isla Verde, the Blue Dolphin offers one of the best views on the island. While strolling along the Isla Verde beach, just look for the neon blue dolphin on the roof—you can't miss it. *2 Amapola St., Isla Verde, tel. 809/791–3083. Open weekends noon–4 AM, weeknights noon–2 AM.*

What to See and Do with Children

Beaches.
Botanical Garden, University of Puerto Rico, Rio Piedras.
Catano ferry.
El Morro and San Cristóbal forts.
El Yunque rain forest.
The Hyatt Regency Cerromar Beach and Hyatt Dorado Beach offer chaperoned camps for children during the summer, as well as during Christmas and Easter holidays.
Mayagüez Zoo, Mayagüez.
Muñoz Marín Park, San Juan.
Río Camuy Caves, near Utuado.

Trolleys, Old San Juan.

Villa Coqui Wet N'Slide, A recreational park with pools, water slides, paddle boats, and canoes. *Rte. 763, Km 6, Caqua, tel. 809/747-4747. Open weekends and holidays 9 AM–5 PM.*

4 Sports, Fitness, Beaches

Participant Sports

Bicycling

The broad beach at Boquerón makes for easy wheeling. You can can rent bikes at **Boquerón Balnearios** (Rte. 101, Boquerón, Dept. of Recreation and Sports, tel. 809/722–1551). In the Dorado area on the north coast, bikes can be rented at the **Hyatt Regency Cerromar Beach Hotel** (tel. 809/796–1234) or the **Hyatt Dorado Beach Hotel** (tel. 809/796–1234).

Fishing

Half-day, full-day, split charters, and big- and small-game fishing can be arranged through **Benitez Deep-Sea Fishing** (Club Náutico de San Juan, Stop 9½, Fernández Juncos Ave., Miramar, tel. 809/723–2292), **Castillo Watersports** (ESJ Towers, Isla Verde, tel. 809/791–6195), and **San Juan Fishing Charters** (Stop 10, Fernández Juncos Ave., Miramar, tel. 809/723–0415).

Golf

There are two 18-hole courses at **Hyatt Dorado Beach Hotel** (Dorado, tel. 809/796–1234, ext. 3238) and two 18-hole courses at the **Hyatt Regency Cerromar Beach Hotel** (Dorado, tel. 809/796–1234, ext. 3013). You'll also find 18-hole courses at **Palmas del Mar Resort** (Humacao, tel. 809/852–6000, ext. 54), **Club Ríomar** (Río Grande, tel. 809/887–3964), and **Punta Borinquén** (Aguadilla, tel. 809/890–2987).

Hiking

Dozens of trails lace through **El Yunque** (information is available at the Sierra Palm Visitor Center, Rte. 191, Km 11.6). You can also hit the trails in **Río Abajo Forest** (south of Arecibo) and **Toro Negro Forest** (east of Adjuntas). Each reserve has a ranger station.

Horseback Riding

Beach-trail rides can be arranged at **Palmas del Mar Equestrian Center** (Palmas del Mar Resort, Humacao, tel. 809/852–4785). Take to the rainforest foothills trails, as well as the beaches, through **Hacienda Carabali** (tel. 809/793–8585).

Tennis

There are 17 lighted courts at **San Juan Central Park** (Cerra St. exit on Rte. 2, tel. 809/722–1646), 6 lighted courts at the **Caribe Hilton Hotel** (Puerta de Tierra, tel. 809/721–0303, ext. 1730), 8 courts, 4 lighted, at **Carib Inn** (Isla Verde, tel. 809/791–3535, ext. 6), and 2 lighted courts at the **Condado Plaza Hotel** (Condado, tel. 809/721–1000, ext. 1775). Out on the island, there are 14 courts, 2 lighted, at **Hyatt Regency Cerromar Beach Hotel** (Dorado, tel. 809/796–1234, ext. 3040), 7 courts at the **Hyatt Dorado Beach Hotel** (Dorado, tel. 809/796–1234, ext. 3220), 20 courts, 2 lighted, at **Palmas del Mar Resort** (Humacao, tel. 809/852–6000, ext. 51), 3 lighted courts at the **Mayagüez Hilton Hotel** (Mayagüez, tel. 809/831–7575, ext. 2150), and 4 lighted courts at **Punta Borinquén** (Aguadilla, tel. 809/891–8778).

Spectator Sports

Baseball

If you have a post–World Series letdown, you can fly down to the island, where the season runs October–April. Many major-league ball-players in the United States made their start in Puerto Rico's baseball league and some return home in the off-season to hone their skills. Stadiums are in San Juan, Santurce, Ponce, Caguas, Arecibo, and Mayagüez. Contact the Tourist Office for details or call **Professional Baseball of Puerto Rico** (tel. 809/765–6285).

Cockfighting

It's the national sport of Puerto Rico, but it's not for the faint of heart. If you're curious about cockfights, head for **Club Gallístico.** *Rte. 37, Km 1.5, Isla Verde, tel. 809/791–6005. Open Sat. 1–7.*

Horse Racing

Races are run year-round at **El Comandante Racetrack.** On race days the dining rooms open at 12:30 PM. *Rte. 3, Km 15.3, Canovanas, tel. 809/724–6060. Open Wed., Fri., Sun., and holidays.*

Water Sports

Sunbathing

Before abandoning yourself to the pleasures of the tropics, you would be well advised to take precautions against the ravages of its equatorial sun. Be sure to use a sunscreen with a high sun-protection factor, or SPF (an SPF of under 15 offers little protection); if you're engaging in water sports, be sure the sunscreen is waterproof. At this latitude, the safest hours for sunbathing are 4–6 PM, but even during these hours it is wise to limit exposure during your first few days to short intervals of 15–20 minutes. Keep your system plied with fruit juices and water; avoid coffee, tea, and alcohol, which have a dehydrating effect on the body.

Touring the island in an open Jeep or dangling an arm out of a car window can also expose you to sunburn, so be sure to use sunscreen. If you have permed or color-treated hair, you may wish to use a sun-protective gel to keep it from becoming brittle; if you have a bald head, apply sunscreen. While snorkeling, *always* wear a T-shirt and apply sunscreen to protect the top and backs of your thighs form "duck burn."

Swimming

Any resort you visit is likely to offer a variety of swimming experiences, depending on which side of the island you choose.

The calm, leeward Caribbean side of most islands has the safest and most popular beaches for swimming. There are no big waves, there is little undertow, and the saltwater—which buoys the swimmer or snorkeler—makes staying afloat almost effortless.

The windward, or Atlantic, side of the islands, however, is a different story: Even strong, experienced swimmers should exercise caution here. The ocean waves are tremendously powerful and can be rough to the point of being dangerous; unseen currents, strong undertows, and uneven, rocky bottoms may scuttle the novice. Some beaches post signs or flags daily to alert swimmers to the water conditions. Pay attention to them! Where there are no flags, limit your water sports to wading and sunbathing.

Swimmers on these islands must also be aware of underwater rocks, reefs, shells, and sea urchins—small, spike-covered creatures whose spines, while not fatal, can cause very painful punctures if you step on them, even through snorkel fins. Moray eels, which are harmless unless provoked, almost never leave the crevices they live in. But don't *ever* poke at one, or even point closely at them—they're lightning-fast and may mistake your finger for a predator. It's possible to receive a minor cut while swimming and not feel it until you're out of the water, so make a habit of checking yourself over after leaving the beach. If you do get a small cut from a broken glass or shell, clean it immediately with soap and water.

Nike, Inc. now manufactures an athletic shoe for wear in water sports. The Aqua Sock, a lightweight slip-on shoe with a waffle rubber outsole and Spandex mesh upper, offers protection from rocky beaches and underwater hazards such as coral and broken shells, and cushions the foot against the impact of windsurfing. It floats, is unaffected by salt and chlorine, and dries quickly.

How much truth is there to the old saw that you should wait an hour after eating before going for a swim? According to Mark Pittman, MD, Chief of Sports Medicine at the Hospital for Joint Diseases in New York city, blood travels from the muscles to the intestines after a meal to absorb the digesting food. This leaves the muscles "cold" and more likely to cramp. It is safe to float or dogpaddle after a light lunch, but save the Olympic lap-swimming for later. *Never* dive, particularly from a boat or cliff, without checking the depth of the water the bottom conditions. And even when the Caribbean is mirror-calm, never run blindly into the water, even if the beach is familiar. Changes in the tide can turn what is a sandy bottom yesterday into a collection of broken shells today.

Few beaches or pools in the Caribbean—even those at the best hotels—are protected by life-guards, so you and your children swim at your own risk.

Sharks More than a decade after the release of the film *Jaws*, shark phobia endures. Sharks *are* among the fish that populate Caribbean waters; they can swim in water as shallow as three feet and are attracted by the splashing of swimmers. But there are only about a dozen shark attacks reported each year worldwide, and most of these take place off the coasts of California and Florida. You are unlikely to see a shark while swimming or diving in the Caribbean, especially if you spot dolphins nearby. The dolphin is a natural enemy of the shark, and will attack its most vulnerable points—the gills and the tip of the nose—so sharks steer clear of them.

Snorkeling and Scuba Diving

Snorkeling Snorkeling requires no special skills, and most hotels that rent equipment have a staff member or, at the very least, a booklet offering instruction in snorkeling basics.

As with any water sport, it's never a good idea to snorkel alone, especially if you're out of shape. You don't have to be a great swimmer to snorkel, but occassionally currents come up that require stamina.

The four dimensions as we know them seem altered underwater. Time seems to slow and stand still, so wear a water-resistant watch and let someone on land know when to expect you back. Your sense of direction may also fail you when you're submerged. Many a vacationer has ended up half a mile or more from shore—which isn't a disaster unless you're already tired, chilly, and it's starting to get dark.

Remember that taking souvenirs—shells, pieces of coral, interesting rocks—is forbidden.

Many reefs are legally protected marine parks, where removal of living shells is prohibited because it upsets the ecology. Because it is impossible to tell a living shell from a dead one, the wisest course is simply not to remove any. Needless to say, underwater is also not the place to discard your cigarette packs, gum wrappers, or any other litter.

Good snorkel equipment isn't cheap, and you may not like the sport once you've tried it, so get some experience with rented equipment, which is always inexpensive, before investing in quality masks, fins, and snorkel. The best prices for gear, as you might imagine, are not to be found at seaside resorts.

Scuba Diving Diving is America's fastest-growing sport. While scuba (which stands for *s*elf-contained *u*nderwater *b*reathing *a*pparatus) looks and is surpisingly simple, *phone your physician before your vacation and make sure that you have no condition that should prevent you from diving!* Possibilities include common colds and other nasal infections, which can be worsened by diving, and ear infection, which can be worsened and cause underwater vertigo as well. Asthmatics can usually dive safely but must have their doctor's okay. A full checkup is an excellent idea, especially if you're over 30. Since it can be dangerous to travel on a plane after diving, you should schedule both your diving courses and travel plans accordingly.

At depths of below 30 feet, all sorts of physiological and chemical changes take place in the body in reponse to an increase in water pressure, so learning to dive with a reputable instructor is a must. Nitrogen, for example, which ordinarily escapes the body through respiration, forms bubbles in the diver's bloodstream. If the diver resurfaces at a rate of more than one foot per second, these nitrogen bubbles may accumulate; the severe joint pains caused by this process are known as "the bends." If the nitrogen bubbles travel to your heart or brain, the result can be fatal.

In addition to training you how to resurface slowly enough, a qualified instructor can teach you to read "dive tables," the charts that calculate how long you can safely stay at certain depths. Many instructors supplement these charts with underwater computers that continuously monitor nitrogen, depth, and other information.

The ideal way to learn this sport is to take a resort course once you've arrived at your Caribbean destination. The course will usually consist of two to three hours of instruction on land, with time spent in a swimming pool or waist-deep water to get used to the mouthpiece and hose (known as the regulator) and the mask. A shallow 20-foot dive from a boat or beach, closely supervised by the instructor, follows.

Successful completion of this introductory course may prompt you to earn a certification card—often called a C-card—from one of the major accredited diving organizations: NADI (National Association of Diving Instructors), CMAS (Confederation Mondiale des Activities Subaquatiques, which translates into World Underwater Federation), NASE (National Association of Scuba Educators), or PADI (Professional Association of Diving Instructors). PADI offers a free list of training facilities; write PADI for information (Box 24011, Santa Ana, CA 92799).

The more advanced Openwater I certification course takes five or six sessions—once a day at a beach hotel, or once a week at a YMCA or school pool back home. You must be able to swim a certain distance to qualify, even if it's dogpaddling. The course requires about 20 hours of classroom work, followed by a written test covering use of dive gear, basic skills and safety measures, and basic rescue techniques. Underwater skills are also practiced and tested.

A certification course will keep you very busy and pleasantly tired for most of your vacation. If your travel plans include a great deal of sightseeing as well, you'll have little time left to relax. You may wish to complete the classroom instruction and basic skills training at your hometown YMCA, for example, then do your five required open-water dives on vacation.

Unfortunately, there are a few disreputable individuals who may try to assure you that they can teach you everything you need to know about diving even though they aren't certified instructors. DON'T BELIEVE IT! Reputable diving shops proudly display their association with the organizations mentioned above. If you have any doubt, ask to see evidence of accreditation. Legitimate instructors will happily show you their credentials and will insist on seeing *your* C-card before a dive.

Keep in mind that your presence can easily damage the delicate underwater ecology. By standing on the bottom you can break fragile coral that took centuries to grow. Many reefs are legally protected marine parks; spearfishing or taking living shells and coral is rude and destructive, and often strictly prohibited. When in doubt, remember the diver's caveat: "Take only pictures, leave only bubbles."

Snorkeling and scuba-diving instruction and equipment rentals are available at **Caribbean School of Aquatics** and **Calypso Watersports** (*see* Boating and Sailing, below), **Coral Head Divers** (Marina de Palmas, Palmas del Mar Resort, Humacao, tel. 809/850-7208), **Cueva Submarina Training Center** (Plaza Cooperativa, Isabela, tel. 809/872-3903), **Caribe Aquatic Adventure** (*see* Boating and Sailing, below), **Castillo Watersports** (*see* Boating and Sailing, below), **Jack Becker's Spread Eagle** (Villa Marina Yacht Harbor, Fajardo, tel. 809/863-1905), and **Parguera Divers Training Center** (Lajas, tel. 809/899-4171).

Waterskiing

Some large hotels have their own waterskiing concessions, with special boats, equipment, and instructors. Many beaches are patrolled by private individuals who own boats and several sizes of skis; they will offer their services through a hotel or directly to vacationers, or can be hailed like taxis. Ask your hotel staff or other guests about their experiences with these entrepreneurs. Be *sure* they provide life vests and at

least two people in the boat; one to drive and one
to watch the skier at all times.

Windsurfing

Windsurfing is as strenuous as it is exciting, so it
is perhaps not the sport to try on your first day
out, unless you're already in excellent shape. As
with most water sports, it is essential to
windsurf with someone else around who can
watch you and go for help if necessary.

Always wear a life vest and preferably a
diveskin to protect your own skin from the sun.
Avoid suntan oil that could make your feet slippery and interfere with your ability to stand on
the board. Nike, Inc. now makes athletic shoes
specifically for wear in water sports (*see* Swimming, above).

Windsurfing rentals are available at **Caribbean
School of Aquatics, Castillo Watersports, Palmas
Sailing Center, Playita Boat Rental** (*see* Sailing,
and Boating, below, for all information) and at
Lisa Penfield Windsurfing Center (El San Juan
Hotel, tel. 809/726–7274).

Boating and Sailing

Virtually all the resort hotels on San Juan's
Condado and Isla Verda strips rent paddle-
boats, Sunfish, Windsurfers, and the like. Contact **Condado Plaza Hotel Watersports Center**
(tel. 809/721–1000, ext. 1361), **Caribbean School
of Aquatics** (La Concha Hotel, Ashford Ave.,
Condado, tel. 809/723–4740), or **Castillo Water-
sports** (ESJ Towers, Isla Verde, tel. 809/791–
6195). Sailing and boat rentals are also available
at **Playita Boat Rental** (1010 Ashford Ave.,
Condado, tel. 809/722–1607). The 600-passen-
ger **Reina de la Bahia** (tel. 809/721–6700) departs from the waterfront in Old San Juan for
sightseeing, lunch, dinner, and disco excur-
sions.

Sailing instruction and trips are offered by **Palmas Sailing Center** (Palmas del Mar Resort,
Humacao, tel. 809/852–6000, ext. 10310), **Calypso Watersports** (Sands Hotel, San Juan, tel. 809/
791–6100), **Caribbean School of Aquatics** (La
Concha Hotel, Ashford Ave., Condado, tel. 809/

723–4740), **Caribe Aquatic Adventure** (Caribe Hilton Hotel, Puerta de Tierra, tel. 809/765–7444, ext. 3447), and **Castillo Watersports** (ESJ Towers, Isla Verde, tel. 809/791–6195).

St. Thomas, U.S. Virgin Islands, and Tortola and Virgin Gorda in the British Virgin Islands do most of the charter and marina business. In St. Thomas, contact the **Virgin Island Charter Yacht League** (tel. 809/774–3944). In Tortola, **The Moorings** (tel. 809/494–2332); in Virgin Gorda, **North South Yacht Charters** (tel. 809/495–5421). The cost of chartering a yacht ranges from $100 to $250 a day per person (all-inclusive, with meals and drinks).

Beaches

By law, all of Puerto Rico's beaches are open to the public (except for the Caribe Hilton's man-made beach in San Juan). The government runs 13 public beaches *(balnearios)*, which have lockers, showers, picnic tables, and in some cases playgrounds and overnight facilities. Admission is 25¢, parking is $1. Balnearios are open Tuesday–Sunday 9–5 in the winter, 8–5 in the summer. (When Monday is a holiday the balnearios are closed on Monday and open Tuesday.) Listed below are some of the major balnearios.

Boquerón Beach is a broad beach of hard-packed sand, fringed with coconut palms. It has picnic tables, cabin rentals, bike rentals, basketball court, minimarket, scuba diving, and snorkeling. *On the southeast coast, south of Mayagüez, Rte. 101, Boquerón.*

A white sandy beach bordered by resort hotels, **Isla Verde** offers picnic tables and good snorkeling, with equipment rentals nearby. *Near metropolitan San Juan, Rte. 187, Km 3.9, Isla Verde.*

Luquillo Beach, a crescent-shape beach, comes complete with coconut palms, picnic tables, and tent sites. Coral reefs protect its crystal-clear lagoon from the Atlantic waters, making it ideal for swimming. *30 mi east of San Juan, Rte. 3, Km 35.4.*

A recently opened beach of hard-packed sand, **Seven Seas** is already popular with bathers. It has picnic tables and tent and trailer sites; snorkeling, scuba diving, and boat rentals are nearby. *Rte. 987, Fajardo.*

Sun Bay, a white-sand beach on the offshore island of Vieques, has picnic tables, tent sites, and offers such water sports as snorkeling and scuba diving. Boat rentals are nearby. *Rte. 997, Vieques.*

Surfing Beaches. The best surfing beaches are along the Atlantic coastline from Borinquén Point to Rincón, where the surfing is best from October through April. There are several surf shops in Rincón. Aviones and La Concha beaches in San Juan, and Casa de Pesca in Arecibo, are summer surfing spots; all have nearby surf shops.

Caution for snorkelers and scuba divers: Puerto Rico's coral-reef waters and mangrove areas can be dangerous to novices. Unless you're an expert, or have an experienced guide, avoid unsupervised areas, and stick to the water-sports centers of major hotels (*see* Participant Sports, above).

5 Shopping

San Juan is not a free port, and you won't find bargains on electronics and perfumes. You can, however, find excellent bargains in china, crystal, fashions, and jewelry.

Shopping for native crafts can be great fun. You'll run across a lot of tacky things you can live your whole life without, but you can also find some treasures, and in many cases you'll be able to watch the artisans at work. (For guidance, contact the Tourism Artisan Center, tel. 809/721-2400, ext. 248.)

The work of some Puerto Rican artists has brought them international acclaim: The paintings of Francisco Oller hang in the Louvre, and the portraits of Francisco Rodon are in the permanent collections of New York's Museum of Modern Art and the Metropolitan Museum. Look for their works, and those of other native artists, in San Juan's stylish galleries.

Popular souvenirs and gifts include *santos* (small, hand-carved figures of saints or religious scenes), hand-rolled cigars, handmade lace, carnival masks, and fancy men's shirts called *guayaberas*. Also, some folks swear that Puerto Rican rum is the best in the world.

Shopping Districts

Old San Juan is full of shops, especially on Cristo, Fortaleza, and San Francisco streets. The **Las Américas Plaza** south of San Juan is the largest shopping mall in the Caribbean, with 200 shops, restaurants, and movie theaters. Other malls out on the island include **Plaza del Carmen** in Caguas and the **Mayagüez Mall.**

Good Buys

Clothing You can get 30%–50% discounts on Hathaway shirts and clothing by Christian Dior at **Hathaway Factory Outlet** (203 Cristo St., tel. 809/723-8946); 40% reductions on men's, women's, and children's raincoats at the **London Fog Factory Outlet** (156 Cristo St., tel. 809/722-4334).

Jewelry There is gold, gold, and more gold at **Reinhold** (201 Cristo St., tel. 809/725-6878) and brand-name watches at **The Watch and Gem Palace** (204 San José, Old San Juan, tel. 809/722-2136.

Native Crafts For one-of-a-kind buys, head for **Puerto Rican Arts & Crafts** (204 Fortaleza St., Old San Juan, tel. 809/725–5596), **Plazoleta del Puerto** (marina, Old San Juan, tel. 809/725–3053), and **Don Roberto** (205 Cristo St., tel. 809/724–0194).

Paintings and Sculptures Popular galleries are **Galería Palomas** (207 Cristo St., Old San Juan, tel. 809/724–8904) and **Galería Botello** (208 Cristo St., Old San Juan, tel. 809/723–9987, and Plaza Las Américas, tel. 809/767–1525).

6 Dining

*by Susan
Fairbanks*

*A graduate of
Cordon Bleu
and Cornell
Hotel School,
Susan
Fairbanks
runs a food
and beverage
consulting
business. She
also teaches
wine courses
in Puerto
Rico.*

Over the past 10 years, phone book listings of restaurants in Puerto Rico have grown from 4 to 14 pages. As a result, there are many new places to try, many off the heavily beaten tourist's path. Whether you're dining at a fine restaurant or picking up fast food in a mall (be sure to visit the one in Plaza Las Américas to see the action), you'll find that every place is extremely busy at lunchtime. Dinner is more relaxed and leisurely, with dress casual to casually elegant; few establishments require a jacket.

On weekends it's common to see Puerto Rican families in their cars sightseeing in the hilly-interior of the island and stopping for a late lunch on a beach or back up in the mountains. Visitors should do as the locals do and go out on the island for at least one meal. The drive is a curvy green adventure that is well worth the trip.

One unique aspect of Puerto Rican cooking is its generous use of local vegetables. Local vegetables include plantains cooked a hundred different ways: fried green, *tostones;* baked ripe, *amarillos;* and fried, plantain chips. Rice and beans with tostones or amarillos on the side are basic accompaniments to every dish. Locals cook white rice with *achiote* (annatto seeds) or saffron, brown rice with *gandules* (pigeon peas), and black rice with *frijoles* (black beans). Chickpeas and white beans are served in many daily specials. A wide assortment of yams are served baked, fried, stuffed, boiled, smashed, and whole. *Sofrito*—a garlic, onion, sweet pepper, coriander, oregano, and tomato purée—is used as a base for practically every thing.

Beef, chicken, pork, and seafood are all rubbed with *adobo,* a garlic-oregano marinade, before cooking. *Arroz con pollo* (chicken stew), *sancocho* (beef and tuber soup), *asopao* (a soupy rice with chicken or seafood), *empanada* (breaded cutlet), and *encebollado* (steak smothered in onions) are all typical plates.

Fritters, also popular, are served in snack places along the highways as well as at cocktail parties. Assorted fritters include *empanadillas* (stuffed fried turnovers), *surrullitos* (cheese-stuffed corn sticks), *alcapurias* (stuffed green banana croquettes), and *bacalaitos* (codfish fritters).

Local *pan de agua* is an excellent French loaf bread, best hot out of the oven. It is also good toasted and should be tried in the *Cubano* sandwich (made with roast pork, ham, Swiss cheese, pickles, and mustard).

Local desserts include flans, puddings, and fruit pastes served with native white cheese. Homegrown mangoes and papayas are sweet, and *pan de azucar* (sugar bread) pineapples make the best juice on the market. Fresh *parcha* juice (passionfruit), fresh *guarapo* juice (sugarcane), and fresh *guanabana* juice (a sweet juice similar to papaya) are also sold cold from trucks along the highway.

The best frozen piña coladas are served at the Caribe Hilton Hotel and Dorado Beach Hotel. Rum can be mixed with cola, soda, tonic, juices, water, served on the rocks, or even up. Puerto Rican rums range from light white mixers to dark, aged sipping liqueurs. Look for Bacardi, Don Q, Ron Rico, Palo Viejo, and Barillito. Puerto Rican coffee is excellent served espresso-black or generously cut *con leche* (with hot milk).

The most highly recommended restaurants are indicated by a star ★.

Category	Cost*
Very Expensive	over $50
Expensive	$25–$50
Moderate	$15–$25
Inexpensive	under $15

per person, excluding drinks and service

Old San Juan

★ **La Chaumière.** Reminiscent of an inn in the French provinces, this intimate yet bright white restaurant serves a respected onion soup, oysters Rockefeller, rack of lamb, and veal Oscar in addition to daily specials. *367 Tetuan St., tel. 809/722–3330. Reservations advised. AE, DC, MC. Closed Sun. Very Expensive.*

La Rotisserie. A bright peach room at its best for Tuesday and Thursday power lunches. Unfortunately, both the food and the service here are uninspired. Flambée specialties include steak Diane and *el pescador* (rice and seafood). The menu also includes Caesar salad, roast duck, and a selection of fresh seafood. *Caribe Hilton, Puerto de Tierra, tel. 809/721–0303. Jacket required. Reservations required. AE, CB, DC, MC, V. Very Expensive.*

Santiago. A very rosy and romantic restaurant featuring nouvelle Caribbean cuisine such as grouper-salmon terrine, pumpkin-tanier-plantain soup, and fresh fish in passionfruit sauce. *313 Recinto Sur., tel. 809/723–5369. Reservations recommended on weekends. AE, MC, V. Closed Sun. Very Expensive.*

La Zaragozana. One of the oldest restaurants around, this adobe hacienda re-creates an old Spanish atmosphere especially for tourists. The ambience is pleasant, with strolling musicians, murals, and vaulted archways. The food and service are tired, though. The menu offers the usual black-bean soup, steaks, lobster, paella, and flan. *356 San Francisco St., tel. 809/723–5103. Reservations advised. AE, CB, DC, MC, V. Expensive.*

★ **Yukiyu.** This is a new restaurant serving sushi, sashimi, and Japanese-inspired specials. The soft-shell crab, shrimp and vegetable tempura, tuna teriyaki, and cod steamed with ginger-and-orange béarnaise are all recommended. *311 Recinto Sur., tel. 809/721–0653. Reservations advised for lunch. AE, MC, V. Closed Sun. and Mon. Expensive.*

★ **Amadeus.** Featuring nouvelle Caribbean food, the atmosphere is sleek Old San Juan with a menu of 20 changing appetizers including tostones with sour cream and caviar, marlin ceviche, and crabmeat tacos. Entrées range from grilled dolphin with coriander butter to chicken lasagna and tuna or egg salad sandwich. Sit in the front room to be seen with beautiful people. *106 San Sebastian St., tel. 809/722–8635, or 809/721–6720. Reservations required. Closed Mon. AE, MC, V. Moderate.*

El Patio del Convento. Since the inner patio was covered with a plastic bubble, El Convento has lost its charm by spoiling the original architec-

Puerto Rico

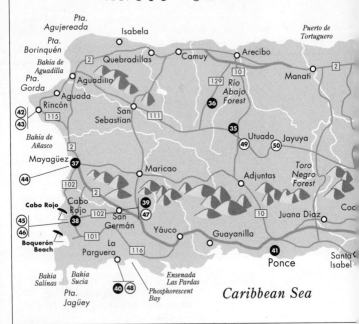

ATLANTIC OCEAN

Pta.
Agujereada
Pta.
Borinquén
Isabela
Puerto de
Tortuguero

Bahia de
Aguadilla
Pta.
Gorda

2 Quebradillas Camuy Arecibo
Manati 2
Aguadilla
10
129 *Río
Abajo
Forest*
36

Aguada
Rincón
42
43
115

San
Sebastian
111
35
Utuado Jayuya
49 50

*Bahia de
Añasco*

Mayagüez
37
44

102
2
Maricao
Adjuntas
*Toro
Negro
Forest*

Cabo Rojo
Cabo
Rojo
102 San
Germán
39
47
Yáuco
10 Juana Diaz Co
45
46
38
101
Guayanilla
Boquerón
Beach
La
Parguera
116
41
Ponce
Santa
Isabel

*Bahia
Salinas*
*Bahia
Sucia*
40 48
*Ensenada
Las Pardas*
Caribbean Sea
Pta.
Jagüey
*Phosphorescent
Bay*

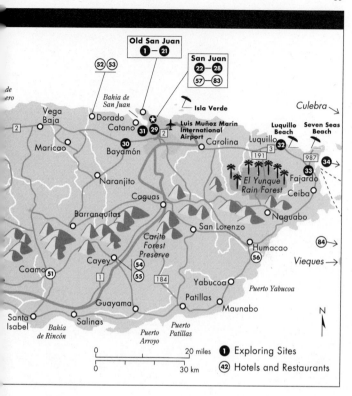

0 ——————— 20 miles
0 ——————— 30 km

1 Exploring Sites

42 Hotels and Restaurants

San Juan Exploring, Dining, and Lodging

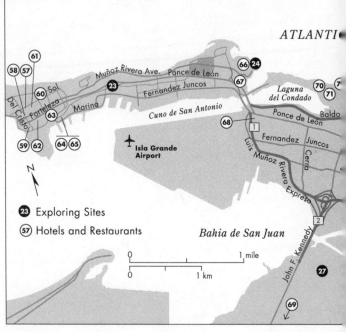

Exploring

Capitol, **23**

Fine Arts Center, **26**

Fort San Jeronimo, **24**

Muñoz Marín Park, **27**

New San Juan, **22**

Santurce, **25**

University of Puerto Rico, **28**

Dining

Amadeus, **60**

Ambrosia, **58**

Augusto's, **68**

Cafeteria España, **82**

The Chart House, **77**

Che's, **81**

Dar Tiffany, **80**

El Nuevo Cafe San Juan, **62**

El Paso, **69**

El Patio del Convento, **57**

Il Giardino, **76**

Kasalta Bakery, Inc., **79**

L.K. Sweeney & Son, Ltd., **70**

La Chaumiere, **63**

La Compostela, **75**

La Reina de España, **73**

La Rotisserie, **66**

La Zaragozana, **61**

Santiago, **64**

Scotch & Sirloin, **71**

Via Appia's Italian Deli, **78**

Yukjyu, **65**

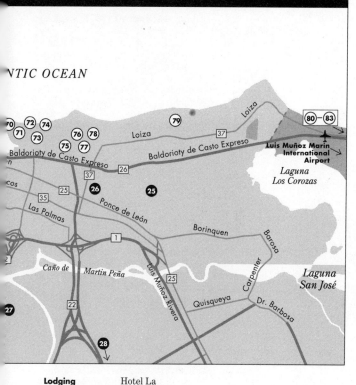

ATLANTIC OCEAN

Lodging

Caribe Hilton International, **66**

Condado Beach Hotel, **72**

Condado Plaza Hotel & Casino, **70**

El San Juan Hotel and Casino, **80**

Excelsior, **68**

Hotel La Concha, **74**

Radisson Normandie Hotel, **67**

Ramada Gran Hotel El Convento, **59**

Sands Hotel and Casino, **83**

ture. The buffet lunch is a cattle train of cruise-ship tourists. The piña coladas are watery. The place is depressing. *100 Cristo St., tel. 809/723–9020. AE, MC, V. Moderate.*

Ambrosia. At the bottom of Cristo Street, the bar serves fresh, frozen fruit drinks while the menu features pastas, veal, and chicken. The daily lunch specials usually include quiche and lasagna served with large mixed salads for good value. *205 Cristo St., tel. 809/722–5206. AE, MC, V. Inexpensive.*

El Nuevo Cafe de San Juan. This café, which features a deli atmosphere, is good for sandwiches and grilled sausages. *152 Cruz St., tel. 809/725–5886. AE, MC, V. Inexpensive.*

San Juan

★ **Dar Tiffany.** This restaurant, just off the lobby of the glittering El San Juan Hotel, is a posh place with palm fronds etched in glass, voluptuous greenery and, yes, Tiffany lamps. Knock back a two-fisted martini from the bar before tackling superb aged prime rib, Maine lobster, or fresh Norwegian salmon. *El San Juan Hotel, Isla Verde., tel. 809/791–7272. Dress: Jackets suggested. Reservations suggested. AE, CB, DC, MC, V. Very Expensive.*

★ **La Compostela.** Contemporary Spanish food and a serious 9,000-bottle wine cellar are the draws to La Compostela. Specialties include mushroom pâté and Port *pastelillo* (meat-filled pastries), grouper fillet with scallops in salsa verde, roast lamb, and paella. This is a favorite restaurant with the local dining elite, and it is honored yearly in local competitions. *106 Condado Ave., tel. 809/724–6088. Reservations suggested. AE, CB, DC, MC, V. Very Expensive.*

La Reina de España. Step into a soft sea-green dining room serving imaginative Castillian cuisine. Chef-owner Jesus Ramiro has just published a new cookbook on Castillian cooking and each of his dishes is artfully arranged and decorated. Specialties include flower-shape peppers filled with fish mousse, a seafood fantasy caught under a vegetable net, roast duckling with sugarcane honey, and a kiwi dessert arranged to resemble twin palms. *1106 Magdalena Ave., tel.*

809/721–9049. Reservations suggested. AE, MC, V. Very Expensive.

Augusto's. Chef-owner August Schriener and his wife Claudia run an elegantly comfortable restaurant featuring classic cooking. Menus change weekly. Specialties include salmon baked in filo, lamb tenderloin with pepper-vodka fettuccine, and veal medallions with smoked mozzarella. The walls are hung with changing watercolor shows. *Excelsior Hotel, Miramar, tel. 809/725–7700. Reservations suggested. AE, MC, V. Expensive.*

The Chart House. Set in a restored Ashford mansion laced with graceful tropical verandas perfect for cocktails, the bar offers good drinks to a lively mix of people. Open-air dining rooms are upstairs, set at different levels. The menu includes prime rib, shrimp teriyaki, Hawaiian chicken, and the signature dessert: mud pie. *1214 Ashford Ave., tel. 809/728–0110. Reservations required. AE, CB, DC, MC, V. Expensive.*

★ **Il Giardino.** Overlooking Condado from atop the Dutch Inn, this roof-garden restaurant's Italian food and attentive service get rave reviews from the locals. Fresh pasta, a selection of veal dishes, and good wines make a moderate meal a pleasure. All ladies leave with a long-stemmed rose from maitre d'/owner Silverio Díaz. *Dutch Inn, 55 Condado Ave., tel. 809/722–1822. AE, MC, V. Expensive.*

L. K. Sweeney & Son Ltd. Brothers Larry and Tim Sweeney have opened a comfortable, casual, and Continental restaurant that overlooks the lagoon lights at night. You have your choice of live Maine or Caribbean lobster, beluga caviar, Norwegian salmon, and Florida stone crab. Thursdays feature a clambake (reservations are a must!). *Condado Plaza Hotel and Casino, 999 Ashford Ave., tel. 809/722–7977. AE, DC, MC, V. Expensive.*

Che's. The most established and casual of three Argentinian restaurants within a few blocks of each other, Che's features juicy churrasco steaks, lemon chicken, and grilled sweetbreads. The hamburgers are huge and the french fries are fresh. The Chilean and Argentinian wine list is also decent. *35 Caoba St., Punta Las Marias, tel. 809/726–7202. AE, CB, DC, MC, V. Moderate.*

★ **Scotch & Sirloin.** Tucked back among the tropical overgrowth overlooking the lagoon, the Scotch & Sirloin has been San Juan's most consistently fine steakhouse. Aquariums light up the bar and the fresh salad bar serves moist banana bread. Steaks are aged in-house and cooked precisely to order. *La Rada Hotel, 1020 Ashford Ave., Condado, tel. 809/722–3640. Reservations required. AE, DC, MC, V. Moderate.*

Cafeteria España. This is a busy Spanish cafeteria serving strong coffee, assorted croquettes, toasted sandwiches, soups, and a large selection of pastries. Spanish candies, canned goods, and other gourmet items for sale are packed into floor-to-ceiling shelves for a cozy, full feeling. *Centro Commercial Villamar, Baldorioty de Castro Marginal, Isla Verde, tel. 809/727–4517. No credit cards. Inexpensive.*

El Paso. Another family-run restaurant serving genuine criollo food seasoned for a local following. Specialties include asopao, pork chops, and breaded empanadas. Daily specials include tripe on Saturday and arroz con pollo on Sunday. *405 De Diego Ave., Puerto Nuevo, tel. 809/ 781–3399. AE, CB, DC, MC, V. Inexpensive.*

★ **Kasalta Bakery, Inc.** Walk up to the counter and order an assortment of sandwiches, cold drinks, strong café con leche, and pastries. Try the Cubano sandwich. There are plenty of stools for sitting, reading, or just looking out the window. *1966 McLeary St., Ocean Park, tel. 809/727– 7340. No credit cards. Inexpensive.*

Via Appia's Italian Deli. The only true sidewalk café in San Juan serves pizzas, sandwiches, cold beer, and pitchers of sangria. It is a good place to people-watch and get something easy to eat. *1350 Ashford Ave., Condado, tel. 809/725–8711. AE, MC, V. Inexpensive.*

Out on the Island

The Horned Dorset Primavera. Lunch, served in a comfortable wicker room, is casual and à la carte. A fixed-price gourmet dinner is served in the upstairs dining room. Enjoy luxurious tropical architecture at its best as you feast on both food and ocean view. No children under age 12 are allowed. *Rte. 429, Km 3, Rincón, tel. 809/*

823–4030. Reservations required. AE, MC, V. Expensive.

La Rotisserie. An institution in Mayagüez, this fine dining room offers the best value for the money in town with its lavish breakfast and lunch buffets. The restaurant is known for grilled steaks and fresh seafood. A different food festival is featured Wednesday through Friday: Wednesday, Italian; Thursday, Latin American; and Friday, seafood. *Hwy. 2, Km 152.5, Mayagüez, tel. 809/721–0303. Reservations suggested. AE, CB, DC, MC, V. Moderate –Expensive.*

★ **El Batey de Tonita.** Set up in the mountains for dining in the cool country air, this restaurant serves local *criollo* cooking with unique specials such as guinea hen fricassee, rabbit in garlic sauce, and crispy "aranita" plantains. *Rte. 7737, Km 2.1, Cayey, tel. 809/745–6312. MC, V. Moderate.*

The Black Eagle. Literally on the water's edge, you dine outside on the restaurant's veranda listening to the lapping waves under the stars. Specialties of the house include breaded conch fritters, fresh fish of the day, lobster, and prime meats that are imported by the owner. *Hwy. 413, Km 1, Barrio Ensenada, Rincón, tel. 809/ 823–3510. AE, MC, V. Moderate.*

★ **Goñzalez Seafood.** Nobody in Puerto Rico makes better crunchy tostones than Rosa Goñzalez. House specialties include fresh shark fillet in wine sauce, *mofongo* plantain stuffed with seafood, shrimps as big as lobsters, and grilled porterhouse steaks. *Hwy. 102, Km 9.8, Joyuda, Cabo Rojos, tel. 809/851–9000. AE, CB, DC, MC, V. Moderate.*

Sand and the Sea. Looking down onto Guayama and out across the sea, this mountain cottage is a retreat into Caribbean living with Kentucky host Hal Hester cooking, playing piano, and singing up a storm. The menu leans toward steaks and barbecues with a good carrot vichyssoise and excellent baked beans. Bring a sweater—it cools down to 50°F at night. *Hwy. 715, Km 5.2, Cayey, tel. 809/745–6317. AE, CB, DC, MC, V. Moderate.*

7 Lodging

Accommodations on Puerto Rico come in all shapes and sizes. Self-contained luxury resorts cover hundreds of acres. San Juan's high-rise beachfront hotels likewise cater to the epicurean; several target the business traveler. Out on the island, the government-sponsored paradors are country inns modeled after Spain's paradors. They are required to meet certain standards, such as proximity to a sightseeing attraction or beach and a kitchen serving native cuisine. (Parador prices range from $35 to $76 for a double room. Reservations for all paradores can be made by calling 800/443–0266 or 809/721–2884 in Puerto Rico.)

The most highly recommended lodgings are indicated by a star ★.

Category	Cost*
Very Expensive	over $200
Expensive	$125–$200
Moderate	$50–$125
Inexpensive	under $50

All prices are for a standard double room for two, excluding 6% tax and a 10% service charge.

San Juan

★ **Caribe Hilton International.** Built in 1949, this superb property occupies 17 acres on Puerta de Tierra and has been further enhanced by a $25 million face-lift in 1988. The spacious lobby is decorated with rose-color marble, waterfalls, and lavish tropical plants. The hotel boasts San Juan's only private, palm-fringed swimming cove. The airy guest rooms have balconies with ocean or lagoon views. The eighth and ninth floors provide VIP treatment. *Box 1872, 00903, tel. 809/721–0303 or 800/445–8667. 636 rooms, including 31 suites. Facilities: private beach, 2 pools, 6 lighted tennis courts, health club, 4 restaurants, disco, outdoor Jacuzzi, executive business center. AE, CB, DC, MC, V. Very Expensive.*

★ **El San Juan Hotel and Casino.** An immense chandelier shines over the hand-carved wood paneling and rose-color marble of the lobby in this sprawling 22-acre resort on the Isla Verde beach. You'll be hard pressed to decide if you want a spa suite in the main tower with whirlpool and wet bar; a garden lanai room, with private patio and spa; or a custom-designed casita with sunken Roman bath. (Some of the tower rooms have no view; your best bet is an oceanside lanai, with or without spa.) In any case, all rooms are air-conditioned, with three phones, remote-control TVs with VCRs, hair dryers, minibars, and many other amenities. *Box 2872, Isla Verde, 00902, tel. 809/791–1000 or 800/468–2818. 392 rooms. Facilities: pool, children's pool, 4 restaurants, 5 cocktail lounges, supper club, disco, casino, 3 lighted tennis courts with pro shop, activity center, water-sports center, shopping arcade, health club, non-smoking floor, facilities for handicapped, complimentary shuttle bus to Condado Plaza Hotel, courtyard Jacuzzi, concierge, valet parking. AE, CB, DC, MC, V. Very Expensive.*

Hotel La Concha. Looking like a large pink seashell, the hotel has individually air-conditioned rooms, all facing the ocean, furnished in contemporary tropical decor. In the main building and the 12 poolside cabanas there are 18 junior suites and 17 one- or two-bedroom corner suites. The VIP suites are on the top three floors. The ritzy Club Mykonos disco is perched right over the water. *Box 4195, 00905, tel. 809/721–6090 or 800/468–2822. 234 oceanfront rooms. Facilities: activity center, water-sports center, volleyball court on the beach, pool, poolside bar, 2 restaurants and lounges, disco, facilities for the handicapped, shopping arcade. AE, CB, DC, MC, V. Expensive.*

★ **Condado Beach Hotel.** Built in 1919 by Cornelius Vanderbilt, the hotel has a pale-pink lobby adorned with bouquets of flowers, a sweeping double staircase, and Victorian furnishings. Guest rooms, each decorated in the Spanish colonial style of the 1920s, have either an ocean, lagoon, or city view. The Vanderbilt Club floors, accessed by private elevator, provide all manner of pampering. *Box 41266, Minillas Station, 00940, tel. 809/721–6090 or 800/468–2775. 245 rooms, including 18 junior suites and 2 1- and 2-bedroom suites. Facilities: cable TV, 3rd-level pool, 2 restaurants and lounges, facilities for* *the handicapped, water-sports center. AE, MC, V. Expensive.*

Condado Plaza Hotel and Casino. Nestled between the Atlantic Ocean and the Condado Lagoon, this stunning resort is two hotels in one, with a Lagoon Wing and an Ocean Wing. Standard rooms have walk-in closets, separate dressing areas, and amenity packages. There are a variety of suites (including spa suites with whirlpools) and a fully equipped executive service center. If that isn't posh enough, you can check into the Plaza Club, which has 24-hour concierge service and a dazzling display of pleasantries. The hotel's Isadora's Disco is a very hot nightclub. *999 Ashford Ave., 00907, tel. 809/721–1000 or 800/468–8588. 585 rooms and suites. Facilities: 4 pools (1 saltwater), casino, disco, 2 lighted tennis courts, 5 restaurants, 7 bars and lounges; fitness, water-sports, and business centers. AE, CB, DC, MC, V. Expensive.*

★ **Sands Hotel and Casino.** Puerto Rico's largest casino glitters just off the lobby, and a huge free-form pool lies between the hotel and its beach. The air-conditioned hotel has rooms with private balconies (ask for one with an ocean view), minibars, and many frills. The exclusive Plaza Club section offers a masseuse, private spas, and other enticements. Like its Atlantic City sister, the Sands books top entertainers—the Club Calypso is the top-name night spot here. *Isla Verde Rd. 187, Box 6676 Loiza Sta., Santurce 00914, tel. 809/791–6100 or 800/443–2009. 420 rooms. Facilities: pool, 4 restaurants, lounge, casino, disco, concierge, 24-hr room service, facilities for handicapped, nightclub, water-sports center, business center, valet parking. AE, CB, DC, MC, V. Expensive.*

Radisson Normandie. Built in 1939 in the shape of the fabled ocean liner of the same name, this oceanfront hotel reopened in late 1988 under the Radisson banner. It's a national historic landmark, done up in Art Deco style, and each room comes with sunroom, minibar, and cable TV. Additional frills and pampering can be found on the ritzy Club Normandie floor. *Box 50059, 00902, tel. 809/729–2929 or 800/333–3333. 180 air-conditioned rooms. Facilities: outdoor pool, 2 restaurants, lounge, ice-cream parlor, busi-*

Puerto Rico

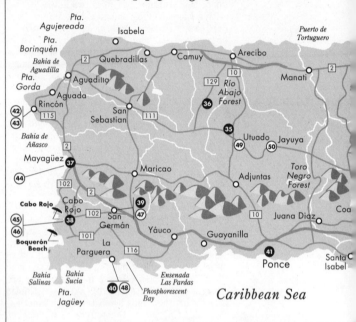

ATLANTIC OCEAN

Caribbean Sea

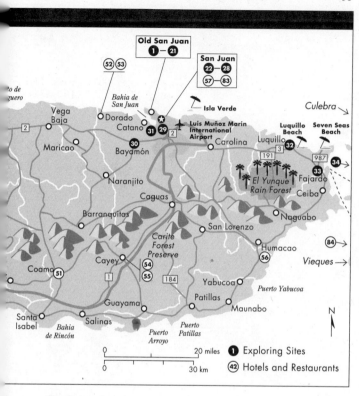

San Juan Exploring, Dining, and Lodging

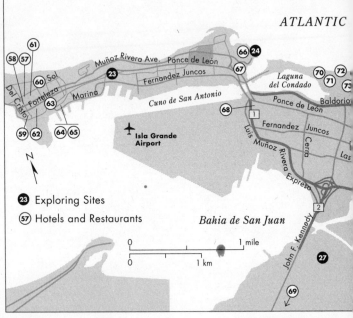

ATLANTIC

Muñoz Rivera Ave. · Ponce de León

Fernandez Juncos

Del Cristo · Sol · Fortaleza · Marina

Cuno de San Antonio

Laguna del Condado

Ponce de León · Baldorio

Fernandez Juncos

Cerra

Luis Muñoz Rivera Expreso

Las

✈ **Isla Grande Airport**

N

23 Exploring Sites

57 Hotels and Restaurants

Bahia de San Juan

John F. Kennedy

| 0 | | 1 mile |
| 0 | | 1 km |

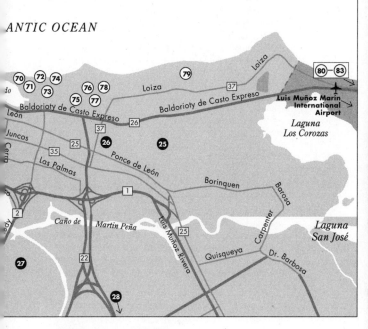

Lodging

Caribe Hilton International, **66**

Condado Beach Hotel, **72**

Condado Plaza Hotel & Casino, **70**

El San Juan Hotel and Casino, **80**

Excelsior, **68**

Hotel La Concha, **74**

Radisson Normandie Hotel, **67**

Ramada Gran Hotel El Convento, **59**

Sands Hotel and Casino, **83**

ness center, health club, water-sports center. AE, MC, V. Expensive.

★ **Excelsior.** Recently spruced up with English carpets in the corridors and new sculptures in the lobby, this hotel is home to the estimable, award-winning Ali-Oli restaurant, which also operates the new poolside El Gazebo restaurant. Each room has a private bath with phone and hair dryer. Complimentary coffee, newspaper, and shoeshine each morning. *801 Ponce de León Ave., 00907, tel. 809/721–7400, 800/223–9815 in U.S. or 800/468–0023 in Canada. 140 rooms, 60 with kitchenettes. Facilities: pool, cocktail lounge, 2 restaurants, free parking and free transportation to the beach. AE, MC, V. Moderate.*

Old San Juan

★ **Ramada Hotel El Convento.** Puerto Rico's most famous hotel, on Calle Cristo right across from the San Juan Cathedral. The pink stucco building, with its dark wood paneling and arcades, was a Carmelite convent in the 17th century. All of the rooms are air-conditioned, with twin beds and wall-to-wall carpeting. Fourteen rooms have balconies (ask for one with a view of the bay). This is a very romantic hotel and an architectural masterpiece. *100 Cristo St., 00902, tel. 809/723–9020 or 800/468–2779. 94 rooms. Facilities: pool, 2 restaurants and bar, free transport to beach. AE, CB, DC, MC, V. Moderate–Expensive.*

Out on the Island

Cabo Rojos **Parador Boquemer.** Located on Route 101 near the beach in a small, unpretentious fishing village, this parador has airconditioned rooms, all with minifridges and private baths. *Box 133, 00622, tel. 809/851–2158. 64 rooms. Facilities: pool, restaurant. AE, CB, DC, MC, V. Inexpensive.*

Coamo **Parador Baños de Coamo.** On Route 546, Km 1, northeast of Ponce, this mountain inn is located at the hot sulfur springs that are said to be the Fountain of Youth of Ponce de León's dreams. The springs were known to the earliest Taino Indians, as well as to Franklin D. Roosevelt,

Thomas Edison, Alexander Graham Bell, and Frank Lloyd Wright. *Box 540, 00640, tel. 809/ 825–2186. 48 rooms. Facilities: pool, restaurant, lounge. AE, CB, DC, MC, V. Moderate.*

Dorado **Hyatt Regency Cerromar Beach.** Located 22 miles west of San Juan at Route 693, Km 11.8, smack on the Atlantic, the Cerromar not only has a lovely reef-protected beach, it also claims that its $3 million river pool—with 14 waterfalls, an underwater Jacuzzi, grottoes, and all manner of flumes—is the world's longest freshwater pool. The completely modern seven-story hotel, done up in tropical style, has tile floors, marble baths, air-conditioning, and rooms with a king-size or two double beds. (You'll find somewhat quieter rooms on the west side, away from the pool activity.) Guests at the Cerromar and its sister facility, the Hyatt Dorado Beach a mile down the road, have access to facilities of both resorts, and colorful red trolleys (free, of course) make frequent runs between the two. *Dorado 00646, tel. 809/796–1234 or 800/228– 9000. 508 rooms. Facilities: airport limo, casino, disco, 4 restaurants, 3 bars, 2 18-hole Robert Trent Jones golf courses, 14 tennis courts (2 lighted), pool, sauna, horseback riding, bike rentals, jogging and hiking trails, airport for private planes. AE, CB, DC, MC, V. Very Expensive.*

★ **Hyatt Dorado Beach.** The ambience is a bit more subdued and family-oriented at the Cerromar's sophisticated sister, where a variety of elegant accommodations are in low-rise buildings scattered over 1,000 lavishly landscaped acres. Most rooms have private patios or balconies, and all have polished terra-cotta floors, marble baths, air-conditioning, and many frills. Upper-level rooms in the Oceanview Houses have handsome king-size bamboo four-poster beds, in addition to a view of the two half-moon beaches. *Dorado 00646, tel. 809/796–1234 or 800/228–9000. 300 rooms. Facilities: 2 18-hole Robert Trent Jones golf courses, 7 tennis courts, horse-drawn carriage rides, horseback riding, hiking and jogging trails, 2 pools, wading pool, casino, 3 restaurants, 2 lounges, water-sports center,*

airport for private planes. *AE, CB, DC, MC, V.
Very Expensive.*

★ **Palmas del Mar.** This is an already luxurious but
still developing resort community, on 2,700
acres of a former coconut plantation on the sheltered southeast coast (about an hour's drive
from San Juan). In addition to private homes,
town houses, condominiums, and villas, there
are two hotels (the Palmas Inn and the
Candelero), and the Ritz-Carlton plans to open a
75-room hotel in March 1991. A number of other
multimillion-dollar projects are in the planning
stage. *Box 2020, Rte. 906, Humacao 00661, tel.
809/852–6000, 800/221–4874, or in NY, 212/983–
0393. 102 rooms, 85 villas, 1-, 2-, and 3-bedroom
suites. Facilities: beach, 18-hole Gary Player
golf course, 20 tennis courts (4 lighted), casino,
equestrian center, 6 pools, 6 restaurants, bike
rentals, fitness center, water-sports center. AE,
CB, DC, MC, V. Very Expensive.*

Jayuya **Parador Hacienda Gripinas.** It's a bit difficult to
★ look for on winding mountain roads, but in due
time you'll find this treasure: a white hacienda
with polished wood, beam ceilings, a spacious
lounge with rocking chairs, and splendid gardens. The large airy rooms are decorated with
native crafts—a very romantic hideaway. *Rte.
527, Km 2.5, Box 387, 00664, tel. 809/828–1717.
19 rooms. Facilities: restaurant, lounge, pool,
hiking and horseback-riding trails. MC, V. Inexpensive.*

La Parguera **Parador Villa Parguera.** This parador is a stylish
modern place on Phosphorescent Bay, with
large colorfully decorated air-conditioned
rooms. A spacious dining room, overlooking the
swimming pool and the bay beyond, serves excellent native and international dishes. *Rte. 304,
Box 273, Lajas 00667, tel. 809/ 899–3975. 50
rooms. Facilities: saltwater pool, restaurant,
lounge, facilities for handicapped. AE, CB,
DC, MC. Moderate.*

Mayagüez **Hilton International Mayagüez.** Built on 20
acres overlooking the Mayagüez Harbor, this
resort on the island's west coast is about a 2½-
hour drive from San Juan. All the rooms have a
view of the sea. A recent $6 million renovation
resulted in completely redecorated rooms, a

new casino, and two executive floors. The hotel is 2 miles from the town of Mayagüez. Also close by are the Boquerón swimming beach, Punta Higuero surfing each, the Mayagüez Marina for deep-sea fishing, seven excellent skindiving spots, and two golf courses. *Rte. 2, Km 152.5, Box 3629, 00709, tel. 809/831–7575 or 800/445–8667. 141 air-conditioned rooms and suites. Facilities: Olympic-size pool, 3 lighted tennis courts, casino, disco, restaurant, lounge. AE, CB, DC, MC, V. Expensive.*

San Germán **Parador Oasis.** The Oasis, not far from the town's two plazas, was a family mansion 200 years ago. You'll get a better taste for its history in the older front rooms; rooms in the new section in the rear are small and somewhat motelish. *72 Luna St., Box 144, 00753, tel. 809/892–1175. 50 rooms. Facilities: restaurant, pool, Jacuzzi, lounge, gym, sauna. AE, CB, DC, MC, V. Inexpensive–Moderate.*

Utuado **Parador Casa Grande.** The restored hacienda is on 107 acres of a former coffee plantation, with wood walkways leading to cottages snuggled among the lush green hills. Each unit has four spacious balconied rooms (No. 9 is way in the back, quiet, with a lovely mountain view). There are trails for hikers, hammocks for loafers, and occasional music for romantics. *Box 616, 00761, tel. 809/894–3939. 20 rooms. Facilities: pool, restaurant, lounge. AE, MC, V. Inexpensive.*

Vieques **Sea Gate.** Occupying 2 acres of a hilltop, this whitewashed hotel is a family-run operation. Proprietors John and Ruthye Miller will meet you at the airport or ferry, drive you to the beaches, arrange scuba-diving and snorkeling trips, and give you a complete rundown on their adopted home. Accommodations include three-room efficiencies with full kitchens and terraces. *Box 747, 00765, tel. 809/741–4661. 16 rooms. No credit cards. Inexpensive.*

8 The Arts and Nightlife

To acquaint the world with the arts and culture of Puerto Rico, "Operation Serenity" was established in 1955. It created a climate in which talent could grow and fourish. The Puerto Rico Symphony Orchestra, a conservatory, and a music school were soon part of the plan. The late Pablo Casals, the famed cellist who adopted Puerto Rico (the birthplace of his mother) as his permanent home, is credited with having sparked this musical renaissance. For many years he was the star of the annual Casals Festival–an ongoing delight.

"Serenity" also prompted the establishlment of the Institute of Puerto Rican Culture, which successfully afflected a renaissance of appreciation of the island's creations in folklore, music, sculpture, painting, theater—the last through an annual theater festival. The Institute is bringing back the past—refurbishing old churches and historic landmarks, building museums, and supervising the restoration of Old San Juan's lovely Spanish buildings. At least a dozen professional galleries are now open in the old city, and a dozen or more are dotted in communities around the Puerto Rican countryside. the Areyto Folkloric dancers have been encouraged to learn and perform (in costume) the old dances of Puerto Rico in the LeLoLai Festival, a weekly program of folklore, printed in the monthly *¿Qué Pasa?* At the performances, you'll see the *cafetal* (coffee plantation) dances and the dance performed by the Taino Indians at the death of a child. The group does an interesting imitation of the cockfights as well as other typically Puerto Rican events.

¿Qué Pasa? the official visitors guide, has current listings of events in San Juan and out on the island. Also, pick up a copy of the *San Juan Star*, and check with the local tourist offices to find out what's doing.

Music, Dance, and Theater

LeLoLai is a year-round festival that celebrates Puerto Rico's Indian, Spanish, and African heritage. Performances take place each week, moving from hotel to hotel, showcasing the island's music, folklore, and culture. Sponsored by the

Puerto Rico Tourism Company and major San Juan hotels, the festivities are free to visitors staying in a participating hotel for at least five nights. *Tickets can be purchased at the Condado Convention Center, tel. 809/723–3135. Admission: $8 for performances, $15–$35 for performances including dinner.*

Casinos

By law, all casinos are in hotels, primarily in San Juan. The government keeps a close eye on them. Alcoholic drinks are not permitted at the gaming tables, although free soft drinks, coffee, and sandwiches are available. Dress for casinos tends to be on the formal side, and the atmosphere is refined. The law permits casinos to operate noon–4 AM, but individual casinos set their own hours, which change with the season.

Casinos are located in the following San Juan hotels (*see* Lodging, above): **Condado Plaza Hotel, Condado Beach Hotel, Caribe Hilton, Carib-Inn, Clarion Hotel, Ramada, Dutch Inn, Sands,** and **El San Juan.** Elsewhere on the island, there are casinos at the **Hyatt Regency Cerromar** and **Hyatt Dorado Beach hotels,** at **Palmas del Mar,** and at the **Hilton International Mayagüez.**

Discos

In Old San Juan, young people flock to **Neon's** (203 Tanca St., tel. 725–7581) and to **Lazers** (251 Cruz St., tel. 723–6448).

In Puerta de Tierra, Condado, and Isla Verde, the 30-something crowd heads for **Juliana's** (Caribe Hilton Hotel, tel. 809/ 721–0303), **Isadora's** (Condado Plaza Hotel, tel. 809/722–5430), **Mykonos** (La Concha Hotel, tel. 809/721–6090), and **Amadeus** (El San Juan Hotel, tel. 809/791–1000).

Nightclubs

The Caribe Hilton's **Club Caribe** books such headliners as Tony-award-winner Chita Rivera. The Sands Hotel's **Players Lounge** brings in such big names as Joan Rivers, Jay Leno, and Rita Moreno. El San Juan's **Tropicoro** presents international revues and top-name entertainers.

(Young locals gather in the El San Juan's **El Chico** to dance to Latin music in a western saloon setting.) The Condado Plaza Hotel's **Copa Room** does a laser revue, and its **La Fiesta** sizzles with steamy Latin shows. In Old San Juan, the Ramada Hotel El Convento's **Ponce de León Salon** occasionally puts on flamenco shows.

Spanish Vocabulary

Words and Phrases

English	Spanish	Pronunciation
Basics		
Yes/no	Sí/no	see/no
Please	Por favor	pohr fah-**vohr**
Thank you (very much)	(Muchas) gracias	(**moo**-chas) **grah**-see-as
You're welcome	De nada	deh **nah**-dah
Excuse me	Con permiso	con pehr-**mee**-so
Pardon me/what did you say?	¿Perdón?/Mande?	pehr-dohn/**mahn**-deh
Could you tell me?	¿Podría decirme?	po-**dree**-ah deh-**seer**-meh
I'm sorry	Lo siento	lo see-**en**-toh
Good morning!	¡Buenos días!	**bway**-nohs **dee**-ahs
Good afternoon!	¡Buenas tardes!	**bway**-nahs **tar**-dess
Good evening!	¡Buenas noches!	**bway**-nahs **no**-chess
Goodbye!	¡Adiós!/¡Hasta luego!	ah-dee-**ohss**/ah-stah-**lwe**-go
Mr./Mrs.	Señor/Señora	sen-**yor**/sen-**yohr**-ah
Miss	Señorita	sen-yo-**ree**-tah
Pleased to meet you	Mucho gusto	**moo**-cho **goose**-to
How are you?	¿Cómo está usted?	**ko**-mo es-**tah** oo-**sted**
Very well, thank you.	Muy bien, gracias.	**moo**-ee bee-**en**, **grah**-see-as
And you?	¿Y usted?	ee oos-**ted**?
Hello (on the telephone)	Bueno	**bwen**-oh

Numbers

1	un, uno	oon, **oo**-no
2	dos	dohs
3	tres	tress
4	cuatro	**kwah**-tro
5	cinco	**sink**-oh
6	seis	sace
7	siete	see-**et**-eh
8	ocho	**o**-cho
9	nueve	new-**eh**-veh
10	diez	dee-**es**
11	once	**ohn**-seh

12	doce	**doh**-seh
13	trece	**treh**-seh
14	catorce	ka-**tohr**-seh
15	quince	**keen**-seh
16	dieciséis	dee-es-ee-**sace**
17	diecisiete	dee-**es**-ee-see-**et**-eh
18	dieciocho	dee-**es**-ee-o-cho
19	diecinueve	dee-**es**-ee-new-**ev**-eh
20	veinte	**vain**-teh
21	veinte y uno/veintiuno	**vain**-te-oo-no
30	treinta	**train**-tah
40	cuarenta	kwah-**ren**-tah
50	cincuenta	seen-**kwen**-tah
60	sesenta	sess-**en**-tah
70	setenta	set-**en**-tah
80	ochenta	oh-**chen**-tah
90	noventa	no-**ven**-tah
100	cien	see-**en**
101	ciento uno	see-en-toh **oo**-no
200	doscientos	doh-see-**en**-tohss
500	quinientos	keen-**yen**-tohss
700	setecientos	set-eh-see-**en**-tohss
900	novecientos	no-veh-see-**en**-tohss
1,000	mil	meel
2,000	dos mil	dohs meel
1,000,000	un millón	oon meel-**yohn**

Days of the Week

Sunday	domingo	doh-**meen**-goh
Monday	lunes	**loo**-ness
Tuesday	martes	**mahr**-tess
Wednesday	miércoles	me-**air**-koh-less
Thursday	jueves	who-**ev**-ess
Friday	viernes	vee-**air**-ness
Saturday	sábado	**sah**-bah-doh

Months

January	enero	eh-**neh**-ro
February	febrero	feh-**breh**-roh
March	marzo	**mahr**-so
April	abril	ah-**breel**
May	mayo	**my**-oh
June	junio	**hoo**-nee-oh
July	julio	**who**-lee-yoh
August	agosto	ah-**ghost**-toh
September	septiembre	sep-tee-**em**-breh
October	octubre	ok-**too**-breh

| November | noviembre | no-vee-**em**-breh |
| December | diciembre | dee-see-**em**-breh |

Useful Phrases

Do you speak English?	¿Habla usted inglés?	**ah**-blah oos-**ted** in-**glehs**?
I don't speak Spanish	No hablo español	no **ah**-bloh es-pahn-**yol**
I don't understand (you)	No entiendo	no en-tee-**en**-doh
I understand (you)	Entiendo	en-tee-**en**-doh
I don't know	No sé	no seh
What's your name?	¿Cómo se llama usted?	**koh**-mo seh **yah**-mah oos-**ted**?
My name is . . .	Me llamo . . .	meh **yah**-moh
What time is it?	¿Qué hora es?	keh **o**-rah es?
It is one, two, three . . . o'clock.	Es la una; son las dos, tres	es la **oo**-nah/sohn lahs dohs, tress
Yes, please/No, thank you	Sí, por favor/No, gracias	**see** pohr fah-**vor**/no **grah**-see-ahs
How?	¿Cómo?	**koh**-mo?
When?	¿Cuándo?	**kwahn**-doh?
Yesterday/today/tomorrow	Ayer/hoy/mañana	ah-**yehr**/oy/mahn-**yah**-nah
What?	¿Qué?	keh?
What is it?	¿Qué es esto?	keh es **es**-toh
Why?	¿Por qué?	por **keh**
Who?	¿Quién?	kee-**yen**
Where is . . . ?	¿Dónde está . . . ?	**dohn**-deh es-**tah**
the bus stop?	la parada del autobus?	la pah-**rah**-dah del oh-toh-**boos**
the post office?	la oficina de correos?	la oh-fee-**see**-nah deh-koh-**reh**-os
the bank?	el banco?	el **bahn**-koh
the . . . hotel?	el hotel . . . ?	el oh-**tel**
the store?	la tienda . . . ?	la tee-**en**-dah
the . . . museum?	el museo . . . ?	el moo-**seh**-oh
the hospital?	el hospital?	el ohss-pea-**tal**
the bathroom?	el baño?	el **bahn**-yoh

Here/there	Aquí/allá	ah-**key**/ah-**yah**
Open/closed	Abierto/cerrado	ah-be-**er**-toh/ ser-**ah**-doh
Left/right	Izquierda/derecha	iss-key-**er**-dah/ dare-**eh**-chah
Straight ahead	Derecho	der-**eh**-choh
Is it near/far?	¿Está cerca/lejos?	es-**tah sehr**-kah/ **leh**-hoss
I'd like . . . a room the key a newspaper a stamp	Quisiera . . . un cuarto/una habitación la llave un periódico un timbre de correo	kee-see-**ehr**-ah oon **kwahr**-toh/ **oo**-nah ah-bee-tah-see-**on** lah **yah**-veh oon pear-ee-**oh**-dee-koh oon **teem**-breh koh-**reh**-oh
I'd like to buy . . . a map a magazine paper envelopes a postcard	Quisiera comprar . . . un mapa una revista papel sobres una tarjeta postal	kee-see-**ehr**-ah kohm-**prahr** oon **mah**-pah **oon**-ah reh-**veess**-tah pah-**pel** **so**-brehs **oon**-ah tar-**het**-ah post-**ahl**
How much is it?	¿Cuánto cuesta?	**kwahn**-toh **kwes**-tah
Enough/too much/too little	Sufficiente/de-masiado/muy poco	soo-fee-see-**en**-teh/ deh-mah-see-**ah**-doh/ **moo**-ee poh-koh
Telephone	Teléfono	tel-**ef**-oh-no
Telegram	Telegrama	teh-leh-**grah**-mah
I am ill/sick	Estoy enfermo(a)	es-**toy** en-**fehr**-moh(mah)
Please call a doctor	Por favor llame un medico	pohr fah-**vor** ya-meh oon **med**-ee-koh
Help!	¡Auxilio! ¡Ayuda!	owk-**see**-lee-oh/ ah-**yoo**-dah/
Fire!	¡Encendio!	en-**sen**-dee-oo

| Caution!/Look out! | ¡Cuidado! | kwee-**dah**-doh |

On the Road

Highway	Carretera	car-ray-**ter**-ah
Causeway, paved highway	Calzada	cal-**za**-dah
Route	Ruta	**roo**-tah
Road	Camino	cah-**mee**-no
Street	Calle	**cah**-yeh
Avenue	Avenida	ah-ven-**ee**-dah
Broad, tree-lined boulevard	Paseo	pah-**seh**-oh
Waterfront promenade	Malecón	mal-lay-**cone**
Wharf	Embarcadero	em-bar-cah-**day**-ro

In Town

Church	Templo/Iglesia	**tem**-plo/e-**gles**-se-ah
Neighborhood	Barrio	**bar**-re-o
City hall	Palacio Municipal	pah-**lah**-see-o moo-**ni**-see-pal
Main square	Zócalo	**zo**-cal-o
Traffic circle	Glorieta	glor-e-**ay**-tah
Market	Mercado	mer-**cah**-doe
Inn	Posada	pos-**sah**-dah
Group taxi	Colectivo	co-lec-**tee**-vo

Dining Out

A bottle of . . .	Una bottella de . . .	**oo**-nah bo-**teh**-yah deh
A cup of . . .	Una taza de . . .	**oo**-nah **tah**-thah deh
A glass of . . .	Un vaso de . . .	oon **vah**-so deh
Bill/check	La cuenta	lah **kwen**-tah
Bread	El pan	el pahn
Breakfast	El desayuno	el deh-sah-**yoon**-oh

Butter	La mantequilla	lah man-teh-**key**-yah
Cocktail	Un aperitivo	oon ah-pehr-ee-**tee**-voh
Dinner	La cena	lah **seh**-nah
Dish	Un plato	oon **plah**-toh
Menu of the day	Menú del día	meh-**noo** del **dee**-ah
Fixed-price menu	Menú fijo o turistico	meh-**noo** **fee**-hoh oh too-**ree**-stee-coh
Fork	El tenedor	ehl ten-eh-**dor**
Is the tip included?	¿Está incluida la propina?	es-**tah** in-cloo-**ee**-dah lah pro-**pea**-nah
Knife	El cuchillo	el koo-**chee**-yo
Lunch	La comida	lah koh-**mee**-dah
Menu	La carta, el menú	lah **cart**-ah, el meh-**noo**
Napkin	La servilleta	lah sehr-vee-**yet**-ah
Pepper	La pimienta	lah pea-me-**en**-tah
Please give me	Por favor déme	pohr fah-**vor** **deh**-meh
Salt	La sal	lah sahl
Savory snacks	Tapas	**tah**-pahs
Spoon	Una cuchara	**oo**-nah koo-**chah**-rah
Sugar	El azúcar	el ah-**thu**-kar
Waiter!/Waitress!	¡Por favor Señor/Señorita!	pohr fah-**vor** sen-**yor**/sen-yor-**ee**-tah

Index

Personal Itinerary

Departure *Date*

Time

Transportation

Arrival *Date*   *Time*

Departure *Date*   *Time*

Transportation

Arrival *Date*   *Time*

Departure *Date*   *Time*

Transportation

Arrival *Date*   *Time*

Departure *Date*   *Time*

Transportation

Personal Itinerary

Arrival *Date*   *Time*

Departure *Date*   *Time*

Transportation

Arrival *Date*   *Time*

Departure *Date*   *Time*

Transportation

Arrival *Date*   *Time*

Departure *Date*   *Time*

Transportation

Arrival *Date*   *Time*

Departure *Date*   *Time*

Transportation

Fodor's Travel Guides

U.S. Guides

Alaska
Arizona
Atlantic City & the
  New Jersey Shore
Boston
California
Cape Cod
Carolinas & the
  Georgia Coast
The Chesapeake Region
Chicago
Colorado
Dallas & Fort
  Worth

Disney World & the
  Orlando Area
Florida
Hawaii
Houston &
  Galveston
Las Vegas
Los Angeles, Orange
  County, Palm Springs
Maui
Miami, Fort Lauderdale,
  Palm Beach
Michigan, Wisconsin,
  Minnesota

New England
New Mexico
New Orleans
New Orleans (Pocket
  Guide)
New York City
New York City (Pocket
  Guide)
New York State
Pacific North Coast
Philadelphia
The Rockies
San Diego
San Francisco

San Francisco (Pocket
  Guide)
The South
Texas
USA
Virgin Islands
Virginia
Waikiki
Washington, DC
Williamsburg

Foreign Guides

Acapulco
Amsterdam
Australia, New Zealand,
  The South Pacific
Austria
Bahamas
Bahamas (Pocket
  Guide)
Baja & the Pacific
  Coast Resorts
Barbados
Beijing, Guangzhou &
  Shanghai
Belgium &
  Luxembourg
Bermuda
Brazil
Britain (Great Travel
  Values)
Budget Europe
Canada
Canada (Great Travel
  Values)
Canada's Atlantic
  Provinces
Cancun, Cozumel,
  Yucatan Peninsula

Caribbean
Caribbean (Great
  Travel Values)
Central America
Eastern Europe
Egypt
Europe
Europe's Great
  Cities
Florence & Venice
France
France (Great Travel
  Values)
Germany
Germany (Great Travel
  Values)
Great Britain
Greece
The Himalayan
  Countries
Holland
Hong Kong
Hungary
India, including Nepal
Ireland
Israel
Italy

Italy (Great Travel
  Values)
Jamaica
Japan
Japan (Great Travel
  Values)
Jordan & the
  Holy Land
Kenya, Tanzania,
  the Seychelles
Korea
Lisbon
Loire Valley
London
London (Great
  Travel Values)
London (Pocket Guide)
Madrid & Barcelona
Mexico
Mexico City
Montreal &
  Quebec City
Munich
New Zealand
North Africa
Paris
Paris (Pocket Guide)

People's Republic of
  China
Portugal
Rio de Janeiro
The Riviera (Fun on)
Rome
Saint Martin &
  Sint Maarten
Scandinavia
Scandinavian Cities
Scotland
Singapore
South America
South Pacific
Southeast Asia
Soviet Union
Spain
Spain (Great Travel
  Values)
Sweden
Switzerland
Sydney
Tokyo
Toronto
Turkey
Vienna
Yugoslavia

Special-Interest Guides

Health & Fitness
  Vacations
Royalty Watching

Selected Hotels of
  Europe

Selected Resorts and
  Hotels of the U.S.
Shopping in Europe

Skiing in North America
Sunday in New York